BREAK
THROUGH

A story of freedom from the pain of
depression and mental illness

JOHN & RITA HELVADJIAN

malcolm down
PUBLISHING

First published in 2018 by Malcolm Down Publishing Ltd
www.malcolmdown.co.uk

British Library Cataloguing in Publication Data
A catalogue record for this book is available from the British Library.

ISBN 978-1-910786-25-3

Cover design by Esther Kotecha
Art direction by Sarah Grace

Printed in Australia

DEDICATION

We dedicate this book to our heavenly Father who
lavishes His love on us, giving us His Son to die on
a cross, that we may be healed, saved and whole.
To Him be all the glory and honour.

To our two wonderful sons, Mark and David; you are
amazing men of God! You are both such a blessing to us.

WHAT OTHERS ARE SAYING...

I have known John and Rita for over twenty-five years and have had the privilege of seeing their journey with God and His work in their lives. This story so beautifully and honestly captures the faithfulness and love of God bringing healing and transformation to them and their family.

John and Rita are a father and mother to many in the Body of Christ. They minister Christ's freedom to many out of the deep reservoir of connection they have established with Him and the reality of His work in their lives. Their story will inspire with hope those who are struggling to find freedom and peace, as well as providing a pathway towards the lasting victory that God has made available to all of His children through Jesus.

Matti Koopman
Senior Pastor New Life Church, BC, Canada

John and Rita have 'laid bare' their past struggles in this book and their quest to find freedom and peace of mind. This life's story is honest and frank and it details their day-to-day fight with the enemy over many years, searching to find *hope* and 'the *answer*'.

They offer this *hope* and the *answer* to every reader! With the world and many in the church gripped in mental torment, often with no hope and no answers, John and Rita have brought *hope* and the only *answer* to a problem no man can solve!

They have directed every reader to the word of God which is the *only* answer. I pray all who apply this godly wisdom will find freedom at last!

Pastor Marion Daniel
Founder of Sozo Ministries International

This is a book that should be read by any person who is struggling, and those who seek to help them. There is a line in it that states 'time is not a healer'. Experience from years of helping people through a wide variety of personal issues, shows that some matters must be confronted in order to resolve them. For some people the causes can be inherited, and for many the issues may be of their own making. To become free requires a breakthrough. John and Rita's struggles made transparent through this book have brought them both to a personal and spiritual strength that enables them to assist others effectively. That's real freedom! I highly recommend this book.

Selwyn Stevens, Ph.D (Bib. St.); D. Min.
Best-selling author and President of Jubilee Resources International Inc.

ACKNOWLEDGEMENTS

We would like to thank the many friends who walked this journey of healing with us; who stood in faith, travailed, prayed and loved us. Especially our dear friends John and Helen Hills, who with their unwavering faith lifted us up when we were full of doubt and fear, and encouraged us to fight and keep fighting when all we wanted to do was give up.

We would like to thank our dear friend Beryl Kelly, who gave her time to read each chapter as we wrote and all the many revisions! Her encouraging feedback, insights, guidance and support were invaluable as we worked through our book.

Thanks to our friends Peter and Carol Hope who encouraged us to keep going when we wondered what on earth we were doing writing this book!

We would like to thank Malcolm Down and Sarah Grace of Malcolm Down Publishing who freely gave us their time and expertise in making this book possible.

To our editor Tim Passmore (The Write Flourish) whose help was invaluable in structurally shaping our book, we thank you.

Thank you to all who took time out to read our book and write an endorsement. You have all given us your love, encouragement and support.

And saving the best to last, we thank our heavenly Father who through all life's trials has never left or forsaken us. How great is His faithfulness!

CONTENTS

PREFACE

Where do we start to tell a story that spans six decades and four countries? A story where so many threads came together weaved to create a picture of life, our life.

The Lord started with two threads – us, John and Rita – and along the way He added others. Love, marriage, children, family, church, career, and is still adding. Not unlike so many other people's lives. We were normal, doing normal things, living normal lives.

Then a dark thread was woven into the weave. A thread we did not expect or want. In His wisdom, our loving heavenly Father allowed this dark thread to be woven into the tapestry of our lives. This thread caused the weaving to go in a sudden, unexpected, almost violent direction. The heavy, black cord marred what had been, up to that point, an idyllic picture of family life. We didn't know it at the time, but that dark strand had a name – severe depression with suicidal tendencies. From that time, our lives were never the same.

We no longer see it as dark, but of a different hue, representing the Lord's direct intervention in our lives, changing our direction, redesigning our picture. Without this thread we would not be where we are today, both spiritually and physically.

Spiritually, we are closer to our heavenly Father, firmer in our faith, more sure of who we are in Christ Jesus and know where we are going. Through the love we have experienced from our Father, we have a deeper love and compassion for people who go through suffering.

We pray our story will give people hope, possibly an answer, and bring glory to the Lord. We have incorporated some teaching in order to explain and give readers insight, so they can make sense of what happened.

Physically, we thought we would always be living in London, continuing the same way. A few years after the breakthrough, the Lord imprinted on our hearts that we were not to grow old in London.

Little did we know that in 2006 we would emigrate to New Zealand, and four years after that we would be living in Sydney, Australia. Before the 'Breakthrough' we would not have had the faith to just sell up and move to the other side of the world, leaving everything behind when the Lord told us to.

For six years we led the 'Prayer Ministry' at our church in Sydney. Currently we are planning to establish our own ministry called 'Complete Ministries International'. We have a passion to bring wholeness, especially mental wholeness, to all who seek it.

When we think of where we are now, we are amazed and grateful for the journey we have been on. And we know that we are still on that journey until the Lord calls us home.

'Not that I have already attained, or am already perfected; but I press on, that I may lay hold of that for which Christ Jesus has also laid hold of me.' (Phil. 3:12)

CHAPTER ONE

CYPRUS
My family roots

John

Could there be a more beautiful island than Cyprus? Nestled on the far-east side of the Mediterranean Sea and surrounded by Turkey, Lebanon, Israel and Egypt.

An island where the sun-kissed beaches stretched for miles and the warm, salty water lapped gently against the shore. Little coves dotted here and there, waiting to be discovered. Nearby, the scent of lemons and oranges from the abundance of citrus trees would assault your senses as you walked along the coastal roads in the cool of the day, the olive trees swaying in the gentle breeze.

As evening loomed, looking out for a tavern in the villages was like searching for treasure. Each tavern prided itself in that they and they alone had mastered the art of producing the best food that Cyprus could offer. A waft of smoke billowing out of the charcoal would swirl around the tavern as a signal to all that it was the time of day to stop, relax and enjoy delicious food with friends.

The chef, with only a vest to cover his protruding stomach, would turn the lamb and pork skewers over the hissing coals. The aroma set his customers salivating with the knowledge that food was about to be served.

The kebabs would complement the fresh salads, which were enhanced with olives and chunks of feta, lightly sprinkled with coriander and doused with olive oil and lemon. Traditional dips of hummus, tzatziki, and a carafe of local red wine made the table complete. Also to hand would be chilled beers and Coke straight from the outside fridge. All this would be delicately crammed onto a checked tablecloth, held down by four pegs clamped to the four corners of the table.

Is there a better way to spend the evening than sitting outside under the evening sky, enjoying good food and wine as the sun sets gently on to the horizon?

But those with discerning eyes and listening ears in the 1950s would notice a change in the conversation in the taverns. The discussion was now becoming more politically charged, with less laughter and the usual friendly banter. Dark clouds were appearing over Cyprus changing the warm atmosphere of the people of Cyprus. There was now uncertainty in the community, and the people of Cyprus had social concerns. Inevitably, this uncertainty resulted in gossip and speculation, creating tension and suspicion, especially in racially mixed communities that had once lived happily together. Friendships formed over many years were broken overnight as the community segregated into the comfort of their own ethnic groups.

This once easy-going, beautiful island was slowly heading towards political, civil and social unrest, and it seemed nobody could prevent it from happening.

The looming danger and unrest that was starting to grip the island was not a new phenomenon to the land. Over centuries, and due to the island's strategically desirable location, many foreign countries had wanted to annex the island for their own nationalistic interests. One dominant force that occupied Cyprus was the Ottomans who ruled the land from the mid-sixteenth century to the late nineteenth century. They had, in turn, conquered the island from the Venetians and ruled Cyprus with an iron fist. In 1878, Great Britain assumed the provisional administration of Cyprus; in 1914 Cyprus became officially annexed by Great Britain, and became a British Colony in 1925.

The people of Cyprus constituted both Greek and Turkish-Cypriots with a minority Armenian section. As a result of the 'Armenian Genocide' which took place from 1915–17 under the hands of the Turks, the Armenians escaped and dispersed from their land. Some of these people had settled in Cyprus by the early 1920s.

The Greek-Cypriots, finally freed from their Turkish overlords, wanted union with Greece (a concept called Enosis). Understandably, the Turkish-Cypriots and Turkey were unhappy about the movement for this and vehemently voiced their objections. In 1931 the Greek-Cypriots rioted against the British administration in Cyprus. At the end of World War Two, the British government had squashed all hopes of Enosis and instead offered self-government under British rule to the people of Cyprus.

The British refusal to agree to the Greek-Cypriots' demands for Enosis sent the movement underground, and the National Organisation of Cypriot Struggle or EOKA (EOKA is the acronym of the organisation's full name in Greek) was formed. In 1951 plans were hatched to use violence to achieve self-rule and Enosis.

The nationalist fervour by the Greek-Cypriots led to increased harassment of the Turkish-Cypriots who, in turn, felt isolated; backed by Turkey, the Turkish-Cypriots demanded full reincorporation into Turkey. The treatment of the Turkish-Cypriots by the Greek-Cypriots, together with the push for union with Greece resulted in the Turkish-

Cypriots creation of a paramilitary group called 'Volkan' (Volcano) in 1954.

The British government realised they needed a base in the Middle East to protect their oil interests. As Cyprus was a strategic location for British interests, this meant that the British were not prepared to give up their rule over the island.

This need for a base resulted in further unrest and uncertainty about the island's future during the 1950s.

My parents were living in Cyprus during this time, both my parents being of Armenian ethnicity. At the time Armenians made up the third most numerous group on the island after the Greeks and the Turks.

My parents and their families had escaped from Turkey during the 'genocide' that was carried out against the Armenians between 1915–17.

My father's side of the family took the opportunity to escape from the ongoing oppression and persecution of the Armenian people by the Turks in 1923. Leaving everything behind, they were desperate enough to get up and board the first ship they could which was heading to Cyprus. There my grandparents and my father disembarked to start a new life, taking the few possessions they had escaped with.

My mother's family had similar experiences as refugees, arriving firstly in Aleppo, Syria, where my mother was born in 1930. Years later they finally settled in Beirut, the capital of Lebanon. When my mother married my father in 1948, she had to move once again to Cyprus and start a new life.

The trouble that had now flared up between the Greeks and the Turks must have been a very unsettling and fearful time for my parents. They had moved countries to escape turmoil, unrest and trouble; would history now repeat itself here in the idyllic island of Cyprus, a place where they hoped they could live in peace and safety? Would they be in danger from the Turkish people again as their forefathers were? Even though the trouble did not directly involve the Armenians, the fear must have been real.

It was against this looming storm that I entered the world on a wet and stormy Friday morning. According to my mother, she had spent the previous twelve gruelling hours trying to evict me. I was slow to emerge but, when I finally did, the memorable day was 20th November 1953. The venue was the only hospital in the capital Nicosia.

I have often wondered, now with the medical knowledge of how a baby in the womb is negatively impacted by the mother's heightened stress and anxiety, whether there is a correlation between my mother's emotional state and how, as a person, I always struggled with many fears, especially the fear of death.

However, despite the situation in Cyprus, my memories of early childhood were more of happiness and security than fear and anxiety.

We lived comfortably in a detached house built by Dad in the Turkish sector. A garden wrapped around the house, with various fruit trees sprawled throughout, and a mature grapevine weaved heavily around the wooden carport. It was a fight as to who owned the space in the carport, Dad or the grapevine. The grapevine won in the end, as Dad gave up parking his car in the carport, and used the street as the car's permanent park. We were never short of fruit from the garden. Even the lemons seemed sweet enough for us to just pick them straight from the tree and suck them.

The other major construction was a large chicken coop in the back garden. We were never short of eggs as the hens were quite industrious. A dominant rooster kept them all in line. One of the chickens became my pet, and I grew attached to her. She would crouch down and remain still for me to pick her up and would follow me around. Unfortunately, Mum had other ideas for my chicken because one Sunday it ended up on our dinner table, stuffed and with its mutilated legs pointing upwards. Instinctively I knew it was my pet chicken, confirmed by my mother's guilty expression. Needless to say, Sunday lunch that day was a quiet affair and, I guess, Mum could have made a better choice of meal time. I felt sick in my stomach, made my excuses (which were unopposed) and left the table crying. Later on, in my teens, I became a vegetarian for about a year. Every time there was meat on the dinner table it reminded me of my pet chicken; a part of an animal on my plate that had once been alive and moved around. Even today I find eating meat difficult, especially steak.

As I grew up, I was not outwardly conscious about the underlying tensions that existed between the Armenians and the Turks, but one could sense there was an air of unease between the two communities. Most of the time ordinary people lived together and got on well. My parents did a great job of trying to shield us from the tension, but one day I got into a fight with the Turkish boy next door. He called me *'orospu çocuğu'* ('son of a whore' or 'bastard'). After the fight, the tension was noticeable on my mum's face as she apologised to the boy's mum for my behaviour. I came away feeling cheated – as if the fight was my fault. It was so unfair.

However, I could sense the fear in my mother's voice; she did not want any conflict with the neighbour over this skirmish. Her fear was symbolic of the mistrust between the two communities; the Armenians were always subservient to the Turks after being conquered by them. Inevitably, the tension and fear that existed in the neighbourhood also became part of my psychological makeup. I grew up always being overtly alert to dangers around me and having a negative attitude about taking a risk. I realise now how this impacted me in the future and in my relationships.

My mother was the most significant person in my life; Dad always seemed absent and busy working hard. He owned a small electrical shop and was also the senior pastor of the Armenian Evangelical Church in Nicosia. If he wasn't at work in the shop, he would be preaching and visiting members of his congregation. We never seemed to lack anything, due to my dad's industrious and positive attitude to life.

We were a close-knit family, made up of Dad, Mum, my older sister Mary, my younger sister Hilda and Grandma from my dad's side.

I was known as a mischievous child and continually teased my sisters. In turn, my sisters always seemed to get me into trouble with my parents. Whenever I was naughty Mum's usual mantra was, 'Wait till Dad gets home!' Often, by the time Dad got home, we were all in bed asleep (or pretending to be asleep). By then most of the issues of the day were thankfully forgotten.

My sisters' toys fascinated me. I wanted to see how they worked. I remember Mary had a small, working, top-loader washing machine she loved to play with. She would put water in it, cram it with her dolls clothes, then click a button and the drum in the middle would rotate, washing the clothes (or making them wet).

One day, when Mary was not around, I finally managed to get my hands on her washing machine. To find out how it worked, I dismantled it with the help of Dad's screwdriver. When I tired of playing with it, there were bits of metal, springs and washers strewn everywhere. Needless to say, I could not put the machine back together again. When Mary noticed her favourite toy in pieces, I could not understand why she was so upset.

'Mum, Mum,' she cried, 'John's just broken my washing machine!'

Mum responded with a smack on my backside, shouting out, 'Wait 'til Dad gets home!'

If that wasn't enough, one day, when I was about seven years old, I smuggled back from my dad's electrical shop a two-pin wall plug, a length of single electrical wire and various torch bulbs so that I could create my version of a torch. Once the house was quiet and everyone seemed busy, and no one would say, 'John, what do you think you are doing?' I attached the wire to the plug, and put the bulb on the other end of the wire. Convinced this would work, I pushed the plug into the electrical point in the wall. Instantly, there was a loud bang, the magnitude of which I had never heard before. I was thrown back into the middle of the room. It must have been a soft landing as I just shook myself and got up. The bang was accompanied by the loss of all electrical power to the house. It created such a commotion that everyone stopped in their tracks and came rushing to see what was happening. The wooden floor must have saved me from being electrocuted. Mum had to go to our neighbour's house to call Dad to come home and fix the power. Dad must have thought, 'not again'. When he arrived home early from work, he was not happy. I tried to keep out of his way, but soon he confronted me. I don't remember the rest, but I did not quite understand what the fuss was all about.

On rare occasions when Dad was not at work, or preaching his three-point sermons to what seemed to me to be the same old people in his church, we would embark on a day trip up to the Troodos Mountains for a picnic. As far as I can remember, a typical day trip would be as follows.

Dad would wake us up early in the morning and insist we all have a hearty breakfast as it would be a long day. We would load the car with all of the essential food and equipment to make a decent kebab when we got to where we were going. Then we would all pile into Dad's Morris Oxford: Dad in the driver's seat, Mum by his side, Grandma – who occupied more than half the seat – in the back, crammed together with me and my two sisters. I know how a sardine in a can feels!

It was a long, winding journey to the picnic area, with the weighed-down car struggling to gain momentum. On the way there, my usual routine required Dad to stop the car suddenly so that I could deposit the contents of my breakfast on the roadside.

Eventually we would arrive at the picnic area, and I can still remember the smell of the pine forest, the noise of rushing water and having to use the far side of a large pine tree as a toilet. Dad would be the first one out of the car. He would wash his face in the cold, flowing brook and make a noise that indicated to all the others on the mountain that this was his idea of heaven on earth.

On the mountain, we would run and play while Dad tried frantically to get a fire going so we could have our kebabs for lunch. After many attempts, fuelling and fanning the charcoal with little bits of sticks and cardboard, Dad would get the fire burning. This must have been fun for him, as he would often disappear into the smoke and we would hear him coughing frantically to clear his lungs. There was something aromatic about the mingled smell of clear mountain air and kebab simmering over the fire.

When food was ready, as always, I stuffed myself quickly (my wife says nothing has changed), so I could play hide-and-seek with my sisters again. Before the sun disappeared over the mountains, we would load the car up again and journey back home.

Again, I would ask Dad to stop the car so that I could deposit my lunch on the roadside; I was not a good traveller, and this happened every time we travelled to the mountains. Cars in those days did not have seatbelts; if they had, maybe I would not have been tossed around and might occasionally have kept the contents in my stomach for a change. I am glad they don't make cars like that anymore.

Apart from my mother, Grandma was the next most influential person in my formative years. I clearly remember, from an early age, Grandma warning me about our neighbours the Turks. When I was only four or five years old, she would continually tell me how they could not be trusted, and that there was something nasty about them. This had an impact on me and I grew up viewing all Turkish people with disdain.

Although Grandma had a strong Christian faith, she could not forgive the Turks for systematically killing her friends and relatives, including four of her brothers. To this day, the Turkish government has not acknowledged the murder of one-and-a-half million Armenians in the early part of the twentieth century as 'genocide'. This, I believe, is one reason for the mistrust of the Turks, and the lack of reconciliation between the two countries.

Grandma and her family once lived in the town of Marash in the south-east region of Turkey. I remember Grandma recounting stories of how hard it had been, on a daily basis, to survive under Turkish rule. The Armenians were repressed and often lived in extreme poverty. She used to tell me stories of how my grandfather would go out to get food every day, and she didn't know if he would ever return home again.

In Cyprus, my grandparents, like most Armenian families who were displaced, had to be very industrious just to make ends meet. In the early 1920s there was little government aid for refugees and, with mouths to feed, the will to survive became paramount.

They established themselves in Nicosia, where my grandfather made pots and pans and other cookware. However, grandfather died of pneumonia in 1937, when Dad was just fifteen years old. As the eldest of three children, Dad had to leave his education and become the family breadwinner – one day a boy, the next day a man.

Dad once told me that his ambition had been to become a doctor so that he could help others, especially in places where people were less fortunate than him. I never heard him complain about his lot in life or what might have been. Dad was resilient, got on with life, and was always grateful to God for everything. My father was a great role model, something I now appreciate with warmth.

Many years later, when my sister Mary and her family visited Cyprus on holiday, she found the school Dad had attended. Miraculously, they had records dating back to the 1930s and Mary discovered that Dad had been at the top of the class every year he had attended.

For me, school life began when my parents decided to enrol me in the Armenian school in Nicosia. As the only son, carrying the Helvadjian name, it may have been an expression of their desire to maintain my ethnicity.

However, academia was not my forte at that stage of my development. The universal language spoken at that time in Cyprus was English, but my first language was Armenian. In hindsight (which is a wonderful quality), being able to learn English at a regular school with the majority of Armenian children in Cyprus, would probably have helped me academically. Instead, I had to play catch-up with the English language and grammar, thanks to commencing academic life in an Armenian school.

Mary informed me that the teachers used to complain to my parents that I had a limited concentration span. These days, psychologists would probably have labelled me with Attention Deficit Hyperactivity Disorder (ADHD), but maybe I was just bored, wanting to run around and chase the chickens in our backyard.

When I was eight the 'penny dropped' for my parents and they decided to move me from the Armenian school to the American Academy, in the hope of improving my English. Dad was one of the school governors – yet another way he served the community.

I found the move difficult and had trouble keeping up with the rest of the class. I guess the teachers must have been amused at how an intelligent man like my father could have such an academically 'stupid' son.

In the meantime, the atmosphere of conflict once again loomed over Cyprus as the Turkish and Greek factions flexed their military muscles against each other.

This resulted in Nicosia being divided between the warring factions by a narrow strip of land that is still 'No Man's Land' today.

Unfortunately, my father's electrical shop was in the middle of the demilitarised zone. But once again, Dad had heeded the signs and sold most of the stock before the conflict. The shop is still there, visible from a distance. It's a shell of a building riddled with bullet holes. I would surmise that now it provides shelter for a family of rats.

Before the conflict finally erupted, Dad had noticed the increasing animosity towards Armenian families who lived in the Turkish quarter. It was no surprise that families were selling up one by one and moving to the safety of the Greek section. In 1962 my parents sold the family home that Dad had built before he got married. By the time of the conflict, we were safely in the Greek quarter, renting a property north of the river.

Dad had an innate ability to sense danger and take action to protect his family. This was part of how he grew up, 'dodging the bullets' in extreme danger. As a nation, the Armenians were martyred for their Christian faith, lost their land and possessions, lived in abject poverty, had to fight to stay alive and were displaced, moving from one place to another. This experience resulted in my family having a strong sense of self-preservation, motivated by the fear of death. Although our parents shielded us, part of their outlook on life has rubbed off on my sisters and me; we are all experts in risk management, to the occasional annoyance of our partners.

In 1964 the simmering conflict between the Turks and the Greeks finally came to the boil. My father, having been aware for some time of the dark clouds ahead, had transferred money for many years into a bank account in England. So with his 'risk-management' hat on, Dad decided that Cyprus was no longer a haven for his family. He had a younger brother, who had previously moved to England, and decided that we should now join him in London. In the summer of 1964, the Helvadjian family were once again uprooted, not out of choice but out of necessity, hoping for a better life in a new land.

My recollection of the big move is very vague. Through rose-coloured spectacles, I remember the comfort of my daily routine in Cyprus. One minute I had been enjoying life with friends, the next I was catapulted into a strange land and culture called England.

I must admit to having some form of amnesia when it comes to memories of that move, which was probably the way my body coped with the sudden trauma of change. My perception of life in Cyprus was that it had been good. Although the school was a pain, by the age of ten I had become somewhat comfortable with my lot. In contrast, my fourteen-year-old sister Mary enjoyed the move, and saw it as an adventure.

Upon arrival in London, we initially stayed with my uncle Nobby and his English wife Barbara. Nobby left Cyprus in the late 1950s and had since established his own business. My father soon joined my uncle in the company and, using part of the money he had previously deposited in the English bank account, Dad bought a house in Muswell Hill in North London.

My first impression of London was not very inviting. It seemed to rain every day, and the natives of the land apparently thought we had landed from another planet. Occasionally, someone in the street would call out a disparaging remark, which added to my feeling of being unwelcome.

It seemed, in the mid-1960s, that the vast majority of people in England had an anaemic Anglo-Saxon look. Anyone who possessed olive or darker skin, as we did, was seen as an unwelcome alien.

Initially, school was not a pleasurable experience. There was often hostility between the majority white guys and the rest of us, the odd-coloured lot. It was a 'sink-or-swim' type of school, but I soon befriended one of the bullies, which offered me protection.

Apart from my appearance, my spoken English was somewhat different. I had a different accent, and my grasp of the language was not on par with the rest.

When it came to the classes, I oscillated between the 'B' and bottom 'C' streams of my year; I often sat at the back of the classroom so that I would not be noticed by the teacher, and finished the class having learned very little. From my perspective, it seemed that teachers in those days were unable to diagnose someone with reading and spelling difficulties, as I had. Instead, we were labelled as 'idiots'. On top of this, my frustration and confusion were further compounded by my sisters, who excelled academically and would bring home either 'A' or 'A+' results. My results were much lower down the alphabet.

I resented my father for being absent on sports days, the one thing I excelled at. This resentment was worsened when my sisters received private tuition, to further their academic potential, while I received no such help. I am sure there was a perfectly reasonable explanation for this but, to this day, I cannot fully comprehend it.

Teachers played a significant part in my development. Mr Jones, a geography teacher who was mad on rugby, would often start the lesson by having us read and copy a section of our textbook. He would disappear for half an hour, and then come back to talk about his favourite subject: rugby. I kid you not!

Another teacher told me that I would 'never amount to much in life' – such a caring attitude. This had the opposite effect on me and, for once, I was not going to accept the teacher's 'expert' opinion. In my anger I inwardly vowed, 'I will show that idiot,' and that vow propelled me from then on to strive to be someone of importance, so that I could shove those words right back down his throat. From then on, if someone opposed me or said I was not capable of doing something, I wanted to prove them wrong. Embarking on such a journey was often uncomfortable. Sometimes I was like a square peg trying to fit through a round hole, determined to succeed at all costs, even if it proved uncomfortable, or outside my capacity. I have since learned the significance of making inner vows, and how they can bind us to specific forms of behaviour that can be detrimental to our well-being.

Assimilation into English culture proved difficult. My dad was experiencing some animosity from his brother; he was working hard for Uncle Nobby but, as a young teenager, it was clear to me that there was an element of tension between my uncle's family and ours. This created unease, especially for Mum who also had difficulty adjusting to our new environment. Mum's ethnic Armenian background, like Dad's, was one of extreme hardship and displacement; Mum, however, was not as resilient as my dad.

By this time, Mum's family had moved to Canada and the tension between Dad and her brother made her want to move to Canada, to start a new life there, close to her family. She still missed them and wanted to be reunited with them.

Nevertheless, Dad took into account that he had an income in London which fed the family, and that we had established ourselves in our new country. With his risk-assessment hat on, Dad decided that moving to Canada was not worth discussing; it was not an option.

Being overruled by Dad in this matter was a bombshell for Mum. Her hope of being reunited with her original family was dashed. She had already suffered bouts of anxiety; now she was experiencing depressive episodes. A doctor prescribed her Librium for anxiety and heart palpitations. From that day she relied on Librium until she died in 1983, at the age of 53, from cancer.

Even on Librium, Mum's life went up and down and there were days when she was unable to get out of bed because of her depression. Growing up, I was mostly unaware of what was happening to my mother and often, when I came home from school, she would greet me with a cheerful face.

My parents continued to work hard in the Armenian community. Apart from full-time work, Dad took the position of Senior Minister of the Armenian Evangelical Church in Chiswick, London, and they were both active in various Armenian charities that sent money to churches and orphanages in Armenia.

I remember when I was thirteen or fourteen years old, having to accompany the rest of the family every Sunday to Dad's church in Chiswick. That was, on average, a forty-five-minute drive. Instead of spending the day having fun or relaxing, I had to listen to Dad preach his three-point sermon.

I *hated* Sundays; I hated having to sit through a service and hear about a God with whom I could not connect. I could not see the point of praying, reading the Bible, or talking to other Christians who seemed to smile at me permanently. In those days, children in church were to be seen and not heard. I was always being told off for fidgeting and restlessness. Church was not a fun experience and I decided that, if this was what it meant to be a Christian, I did not want any part of it.

After the service, we were often invited to someone's house for tea. It was a family tradition that we be on our best behaviour when visiting church friends. After a few hours, in the late afternoon or early evening, we would travel back home, only to get ready for school the next day.

When I was fifteen, I met an Armenian guy who was the same age but already six-feet tall. He was big and ugly, which qualified him to be the head of a gang where all the members dressed as skinheads. I joined the group, adopting the same identity as the others in the gang. I cropped my hair very short, bought a Ben Sherman shirt, braces, Levi jeans and a pair of heavy boots.

When I arrived home with my new look, my parents were shocked. They knew about skinheads. They knew these gangs created trouble and now their son was one. This caused them great distress but, in my selfishness, I did not care. Dad confronted me but I told him I did not want anything to do with his religion, and that there was nothing he could do about the gang I had joined. It was a great embarrassment for my parents – the son of a preacher, being in a gang. Looking back, I am saddened by the way I dishonoured my parents and dismissed their concerns.

However, the gang gave me something I had been searching for – a family that valued its members equally. The respect was in the dress code; my skin colour did not matter anymore. We were a mixture of all races, with a common goal to kick the life out of the other gangs, known as the 'Mods' and 'Rockers'.

Gang members looked out for each other. Loyalty was paramount. We hung around clubs and pubs, and we were feared by those around us. I believe the gang gave me my first sense of belonging to a family that valued each other, regardless of academic achievements and ethnic background.

Eventually, at the age of sixteen, I became bored with gang life and was ready to move on. I grew my hair long and became a hippie, finding my identity in something completely different. It was the late 1960s, and everything was about love and peace. Once again, my parents were dismayed. What happened to their lovely, obedient little boy?

In my search for meaning in life I drifted from one experience to another, totally ignoring the God factor. As I reflect on those times, I can see that God had His hand over me. I did not abuse my body with drugs or sex and, remarkably, I never got into any trouble with the police. I remember at one party people were smoking and passing around a joint. When it came to my turn to inhale, I made a split-second decision and said 'no'. That was indeed a God moment, because I must have been the only one in the room to reject the smoke. To this day I have not taken any illicit drugs.

Growing up, I was more interested in football than girls. Kicking a round object in the air seemed less complicated than going through the minefield of pubescent relationships.

However, when I was around sixteen or seventeen I began to view the whole mating game a little differently.

I had a few casual dates in the sixth form, and began to be intrigued by the feminine shape. I remember one girl, Barbara, who seemed to be making a play for me. Something about her made me feel shy. I pretended to be indifferent and played a little hard to get. Eventually she wore me down, and we dated on a few occasions. Nothing came of it and deep down I knew I was not ready for a girlfriend-boyfriend commitment.

There was another girl in our group, Sally, who took my fancy and she was my first real girlfriend. I soon liked her very much and became emotionally involved. When we had been dating for about six months, Sally's friends saw that we were getting serious and told her that she should end the relationship because I was not a Christian. So one day she called the relationship off and told me why, which left me confused. For a couple of days, I was heartbroken. I did not understand this 'Christian bit'; how could someone break-up a relationship because of some stupid religious belief?

I was sad at the loss of Sally, but angry at God. Anyway, did such a thing as a God exist? I wondered how someone like Sally could be so stupid as to believe something that was a figment of people's imagination. This conclusion helped me to get over Sally very quickly.

By now we had just left school, but as a group of friends we still kept in touch and occasionally hung out with each other. One evening James and I went out casually with a couple of the girls we knew from school. One of the girls was Barbara, the same Barbara I had gone out with a few times before.

Barbara was now living in Earl's Court, training to be a hotel housekeeper. She had changed since school; nothing that I could put my finger on, but something about her was different. This time she caught my eye. As I eyed her over, my hormone levels went off the Richter Scale. This was something I had never felt before. I found her physically attractive and now I was the one chasing the prize. The fact that she already had a boyfriend was a minor consideration. I finally wore her down with my attention, and she said 'yes' to a date.

Again, I was on God's radar because Barbara was also a Christian. I would take her out to expensive restaurants, buy the most expensive wine I could afford, even if it were half a bottle, and try to impress her with my worldly knowledge of French claret and the different chateaux in the Dordogne. As my eyes glowed with desire for romance, all she would do was talk about Jesus.

Wherever I went, I kept bouncing into these weird Christians who would tell me about this character called Jesus. I could comprehend He was a nice guy and did a lot of good to people. But this concept of God coming down to earth as a man was just a nice story, and one for those who dreamed a lot. The whole Jesus thing was a bit far-fetched for me, and made no logical sense.

However, one day, when I was at work doing something mundane as one does at work, something touched me in my heart. God was bypassing His foot-soldiers and dealing directly with me. The only way I can describe it is that I felt this tremendous warmth come over me. Initially I could not put my finger on it, and I thought I was just feeling good, or too close to a heater. But this was more than feeling good. I also had a revelation and all those logical arguments I had perfected to confront Christians with seemed nonsensical.

So there among the shelves in the basement at work, I accepted Christ Jesus as my personal saviour. Immediately I felt a love from God that I had never experienced before. It felt like it lasted a few moments, but must have been longer than that because one of my work colleagues called out, wondering where I was. From that moment I felt ten-feet tall, as if I was floating above the ground on a cushion of air. When I met up with Barbara that evening she was over the moon, and from then on our relationship deepened. I knew then that she was the one for me, and that we would eventually get married.

CHAPTER TWO

LONDON
Refugees in the rain

Rita

I have to confess that my real name is not Rita. I was not born Rita or legally known as Rita; I was never called Rita at school, or among my friends. At home I was called 'Ritza' by my father and 'Lulistza' by my mother. Very confusing, I know, but I grew up being able to respond to various names in different contexts.

In truth, on 21st July 1954, a bright, sunny day in Nicosia the capital of Cyprus, I was born Barbara Michaelides. I was welcomed into the world by my Greek-Cypriot mother, Nikki, my Turkish father, Kyriakos Michaelides and, possibly, also by my brother, who was around five at the time.

As for my surname, 'Michaelides' was not my father's legal birth name. He was born Kemal Mustapha so, technically, I should have been Barbara Mustapha. So how did I become Rita Helvadjian, nee Michaelides?

We must backtrack and start with my father. Very little is known about his upbringing in Cyprus as he never wanted to talk much about it. What we do know is that he was born a Muslim in Cyprus on 2nd February 1919. His father had a couple of wives: one where he lived and one in the next village. Dad also had a few sisters. At that time Cyprus was under British rule and, at the age of sixteen, my father, who had been virtually abandoned by this time, wanted to enlist in the British army. It seemed a pretty good option for him. He would be fed, watered, paid and it would get him off the streets. The only problem was that the minimum enlistment age was eighteen. Knowing that the army could not prove otherwise, he just lied and said that he was eighteen. In those days no papers were needed, no proof of who you were and, I suspect, the army required men so anyone would do. When my father died on 20th April 1993, we had a small discussion as to what age to put on the paperwork, and his tombstone – we put his actual date of birth.

A few years later, in his early twenties, my father was fighting for the British Army during the Second World War in Egypt. While fighting at El Alamein he had a revelation, which could only be from God, that he was going to die and that he was in the wrong religion. In Cyprus there were only two religions – Greek Orthodox and Islam – so you were either a Christian or a Muslim. If Islam was the wrong religion, my father thought, the right religion must be Greek Orthodox. So one night he pinched a jeep and drove to Alexandria. He went to a Greek family that he was friendly with and spoke to his friend, Emanuel, saying he wanted to convert. Emanuel took him to see the archbishop.

Imagine the scene: in the middle of a war, a Muslim British soldier turns up on their doorstep, asking to convert. The priests were very suspicious, and rightly so. Apparently they thought he was converting because of a woman but he managed to convince them that he was sincere.

Dad stayed with them for three months, taking instruction from them about his new faith. Then he was baptised at St Nicholas Church which was in the garden of a private family, and he was given a new Greek name, Kyriakos Michaelides. A change of name was significant in those times; your name identified you as being either Greek or Turkish. As far as my father was concerned, from that time on he was Greek and no longer Turkish. His conversion and new name had transferred him from one ethnic group to another.

My father, now duly Greek, returned to the British Army. Of course, questions were asked; I mean, you can't just desert your post. The funny thing is that they did not court-martial him but rather accepted his explanation. Rumour has it they even promoted him. How he managed to get new papers and a passport in his new name is a mystery to this day. But it was an age before computers, before databases, even before the need to have birth certificates.

How I regret that I did not take time to sit with my father and talk to him about his life. To ask him about his experiences: what made him convert, how did he deal with the rejection from his family (all but one sister disowned him), what was the British Army's reaction to his return, and so much more. I was thirty-nine when my father died. Looking back, one always thinks there will be plenty of time for chats, but there was also an element of selfishness on my part, as I was wrapped up in my own world at the time.

A few years after the Second World War had ended, my father, now in his late twenties, was working at the British government Census Office as a messenger. There he met my mother, Nikki Kolossides, a beautiful eighteen-year-old straight out of school. According to Mum, he kept staring at her whenever he had to go to her office. One day he told her, 'I love you and want to marry you.' Mum threw him out, but eventually succumbed to his charm. However, the path of true love, as we know, never runs smoothly.

My mother came from an educated Greek family who were not too happy about my father being on the scene. My mother's four younger brothers were very protective of their sister and made suitable inquiries about her suitor. My father had a somewhat dubious reputation for being a ladies' man who was rather fond of alcohol. He was not educated and, once they found out he was Turkish, it was a definite 'no'.

ΠΑΤΡΙΑΡΧΕΙΟΝ ΑΛΕΞΑΝΔΡΕΙΑΣ

PATRIARCAT GREC ORTHODOXE
ALEXANDRIE

Ἀρ. 2250

ΠΙΣΤΟΠΟΙΗΤΙΚΟΝ

Τό, ἐν Ἀλεξανδρείᾳ Γραφεῖον τοῦ Ἁγιωτάτου, Ἀποστολικοῦ
καί Πατριαρχικοῦ Θρόνου Ἀλεξανδρείας δῆλον ποιεῖται ὅτι ὡς ἐμφαί-
νεται ἐκ τοῦ Πρακτικοῦ βαπτίσεως ἀπό 7ης Μαρτίου 1942 ὁ τέως ὀνομα-
ζόμενος Κεμάλ Μουσταφᾶ, γεννηθείς ἐν Λευκωσίᾳ τῇ 2ᾳ Φεβρουαρίου 1919,
προερχόμενος ἐκ τοῦ Μουσουλμανισμοῦ, καταγόμενος ἐκ Λευκωσίας τῆς
Κύπρου, αἰτήσει αὐτοῦ καί κατόκιν τῆς νενομισμένης κατηχήσεως ἐγένετο
δεκτός εἰς τούς κόλπους τῆς καθ᾽ ἡμᾶς Ἐκκλησίας, βαπτισθείς δέ κατά
τάς σεπτάς διακελεύσεις τῆς Μιᾶς, Ἁγίας, Καθολικῆς καί Ἀποστολικῆς
Ἐκκλησίας ἐν Ἰβραημίᾳ ἐν τῷ Ἱερῷ Ναῷ τῶν Ταξιαρχῶν, ἱερουργοῦντος
τοῦ Ἐδλ.Πρεσβυτέρου Γεωργίου Ζογανᾶ τῇ 7ῃ Μαρτίου 1942, ἔλαβε τό ὄνομα
ΚΥΡΙΑΚΟΣ ἐξελεξάμενος καί τό ἐπώνυμον ΜΙΧΑΗΛΙΔΗΣ, ὡς ἀναδόχων παριστα-
μένων τῶν Δ. Οἰκονομίδη ἐκ Λευκωσίας καί Ἐμμανουήλ Ὀρτάκη, ἐκ Σμύρ-
νης.

Εἰς πίστωσιν δίδεται τό παρόν τῇ αἰτήσει του.
Ἐν Ἀλεξανδρείᾳ τῇ 16ῃ Ἰουλίου 1946

Ο ΓΕΝΙΚΟΣ ΠΑΤΡΙΑΡΧΙΚΟΣ ΕΠΙΤΡΟΠΟΣ

The Baptismal Certificate

SYDNEY
TRANSLATION SERVICES

Australia: +61 (0) 2 8006 8007
enquiry@sydneytranslation.com.au
Level 40, North Point Tower, 100 Miller Street
North Sydney NSW 2060

PATRIARCHATE OF ALEXANDRIA
GREEK ORTHODOX PATRIARCHATE
ALEXANDRIA

No. 2250

CERTIFICATE

The Office of the Most Holy Apostolic and Patriarchal Throne of Alexandria at Alexandria, certifies that as appearing in the Baptism Certificate Minutes dated 7th March 1942, the formerly named person Kemal Moustafa, born at Nicosia on 2nd February 1919, being a former follower of the Islamic faith, originally hailing from Nicosia Cyprus, upon his application and after undergoing the authorised *catechism was accepted into the fold of our Church, was baptised in accordance with the venerable orders of Our Holy Orthodox-Catholic and Apostolic Church at *Ivraimia at the Holy Church of Taxiarchon, the Sacraments of the Baptism Ceremony were performed by the Very Reverend Georgios Zoganas on 7th March 1942, and he was assigned the given name KYRIAKOS as selected and the surname MICHAILIDIS, the godparents present being D. Oikonomidis from Nicosia and Emmanouil Ortakis from Smyrni.

This certificate is issued upon his application.

At Alexandria 16th July 1946

THE GENERAL PATRIARCHATE OFFICER
(signature)

Translator's Notes:
*Catechism – Christian teaching by question and answer.
*Ivraimia – Modern day Ebreem which is a suburb of Alexandria Egypt.
Affixed on the original document is the seal of the Patriarchate of Alexandria and one service stamp duty.
Translator's Certification:
I, *Dennis Dellas* NAATI accredited translator (NAATI No: CPN4EJ56L), certify that the above document is a true and correct translation from the *Greek* language into the *English* language of a *Certificate* relating to *Kyriakos Michailidis former Kemal Moustafa*.

DENNIS DELLAS
CPN4EJ56L
GREEK <-> ENGLISH
VALID TO 1/03/2021
SIGNATURE:
TRANSLATION DATE: 1/5/18
CERTIFIED TRANSLATOR

Translation of Baptismal Certificate

My father told my mother that she was of legal age and did not need their approval, so Mum took her birth certificate and they eloped, getting married on 11th May 1947. A couple of years later my brother Andrew was born and I followed a few years after that.

Now you know how I received my surname, but what of my first name? This is a little easier to explain. My Greek name, if translated into English, would sound something like 'Barbararitza', so I was called 'Ritza' for short, but legally I was Barbara.

Because my parents had eloped, my mother did not receive any trousseau, wedding gifts or money. They started married life sleeping in the office, and then they moved to rented accommodation. Both my parents worked hard and, early in 1957, they managed to buy land in Ayios Domedios, Nicosia.

First, they built a one-bedroom house and subsequently extended it to a three-bedroom place. I had a nanny to look after me, and my mother had help in the house. According to my mother, I was a 'lovely little thing', chubby, with a full head of shocking blonde hair. Going to the mountains during the summer, the beaches, the beautiful food and the glorious weather, made our life easy and gentle. My brother remembers that when he was meant to be having his afternoon nap, my father would knock outside his window, and they would escape together to go and fly kites – unbeknown to my mother.

My mother and brother have told me that we had a lovely life in Cyprus, but I have no memories of that time. I know only what I have been told or have seen in pictures. When I was four years old we were violently and rudely shaken from our quiet, idyllic life – an event which caused me, I believe, to suffer from something I can only describe as 'traumatic amnesia'.

Our quiet, idyllic life came to an abrupt end in 1958 when trouble flared up in Cyprus between the Turks and the Greeks. We were a casualty of that crisis. My father had received a letter signed 'Volkan' – later known as the Turkish Resistance Organisation – a paramilitary group whose aim was to promote the partition and the annexation of Cyprus to Turkey. The letter stated that they were going to kill him, and us, because he had converted to Christianity.

I often ask myself, 'How did they know? Why him? Surely he was not the only person in the whole of Cyprus to have converted.' My father was just an ordinary man, with an ordinary family, living an ordinary life. What purpose were they hoping to achieve by threatening him? His death would not have advanced their cause. It might have been an empty threat, just trying to cause as much trouble as possible between the Greeks and the Turks. Whether it was an empty threat or not, my parents took it seriously.

My mother tells me that one day she came home and saw my father sitting on the veranda cuddling me. He was crying, and saying that he was going to be killed, and that he loved me. I have no recollection of this event, or of that particular time. But I wonder whether the threat of death that surrounded us at that time subconsciously affected me, as one of the most significant battles in my life has been overcoming a fear of death.

In order to save my father's life, secret plans were put in place to escape to England. We were all British citizens, so England was the logical place to go. My parents quickly packed as much as they could in as many suitcases as they could carry, locked the front door of our house and just walked away. My parents had a friend, Mario Aquiline, who was an engineer they worked with. He drove us to Limassol where we picked up the boat to Marseille, then the train to Calais, the ferry to Folkestone and, finally, the train to Kings Cross station.

Mario had a brother, George, who met us at Kings Cross. My parents did not know anyone in England and had arrived with only a half-crown in their pockets. Only my mother spoke fluent English. If George was not there waiting at Kings Cross, there was no Plan B.

I cannot even begin to imagine what my parents went through: to have a death threat hanging over you, to leave your home suddenly, your family, your security, everything you have ever known, and to run with two small children to a foreign country. Since my mother did not want us to grow up without a father, there was no other option: we had to run. The fears they must have felt, the panic they must have suppressed as they journeyed to England. What if George did not turn up; where would they go, where would they stay with two small children in tow?

Only now, as I write and unpack these events, do I appreciate the sacrifices, trauma and courage my parents had, and I wish I had expressed my thankfulness to my father before he died. I was too wrapped up in my life to think of theirs, to think of the hardships they went through. But children do not fully understand their life through their parents' eyes.

My parents waited anxiously at the station, having never met their friend's brother before, nor even having seen a picture of him. How would they recognise him? My mother told me that as they looked around, a man was standing there, and when he put his glasses on he looked so much like Mario that she knew it was him.

Nicosia 4th August, 1958.

CONFIDENTIAL.

Hon. Establishment Secretary,

Sir,

I have the honour to inform you that due to security reasons I have to resign my post of Permanent Messenger, C.B.S. as from the 5th August, 1958 and leave for the United Kingdom for protection of myself and my family (wife and two children).

The reason is that I have received a letter a few days ago signed " VOLKAN " asking me to leave Cyprus otherwise they will kill both my family and myself.

My gratuity, salary and G.E.P.F. due to me may be paid to Mr. Mario S. Aquilina, Technician, Treasury H.Q., who is in possession of a Power of Attorney.

As I resign my post unintentionally I request you that authority may be given to me to be paid my contributions towards the G.E.P.F. plus Government Contributions.

I have the honour to be,
Sir,
Your Obidient Servant,

Kyriakos Michaelides,
Messenger, C.B.S.

Copy to: Director C.B.S.

Resignation letter

43

George took us to his home and we stayed there for the first few nights. Was he just a Good Samaritan or maybe an angel in disguise? We were frightened, tired and weary, yet despite not knowing us from Adam, he warmly welcomed us. To this day his family has stayed close to ours, and when my sister Nina was born in 1963, George and his wife became her godparents.

My parents eventually managed to find work. My mother was educated and fluent in English, and found a job in the Accounts Department of a company called Hilger & Watts – makers of scientific instruments. My father, who was not educated and had poor English, struggled to find work initially. Eventually he got a job as a baker, then as a mechanic in a garage, and finally, after three attempts, a job in London Transport. Initially he was employed as a General Hand cleaning the buses. His aim, though, was to be a bus driver and, on his third attempt, he passed British Transport's Bus Driver's Test, and Dad remained a bus driver until he retired.

My brother and I had been suddenly taken from an idyllic lifestyle, where we had hired help, a nanny who took care of us and an extended family. We were transported from a land of sun, colour and warmth to a place of rain, drabness and cold. Instead of having our parents around, we were left alone while they worked 24/7, no hired help, and no nanny – my brother looked after me while our parents worked. We lost our lovely home, surrounded by fruit trees, grounds and space, and were now staying in a cramped, rented flat with no garden.

My brother often told me that, to him, it was like being suddenly whisked from Paradise to Hell, so marked was the difference in our lives.

I have vague memories of one flat where the cooker was outside in the hall, and was shared by all the tenants. My mother was fastidious and would not cook anything without first cleaning the cooker. It must have been so hard for her, who once hired the help in the house, to come home after a day's work to do all those things herself. My parents were starting life, once again, with nothing.

About a year later the trouble in Cyprus had died down sufficiently for my father to return to sell our family home. He went to the office of Archbishop Makarios, who would later become the first President of Cyprus. He told the archbishop of their plight, which, he explained, was because of his conversion. The archbishop listened, and bought our house to give to one of his associates, Ioannis Pissas. Dad sold the house for over 500 Cyprus pounds, which he transferred to England.

In November 1959, with the money from the sale as a deposit, my parents were able to buy a house in Wood Green in north London. It was an old Victorian terrace house with three bedrooms and an outside toilet. It is from this point on that my memories begin. It is as if my life up to that point did not exist; I cannot even remember my first language, which is Greek.

My brother, who was five years older than me, became my surrogate carer. He told me that one day the social worker came to see our parents, asking them why he kept missing school. I am sure he was often frustrated and unhappy with his lot in life. It cannot have been easy for him to suddenly assume adult responsibilities – the carefree life he had in Cyprus gone.

We were left, most of the time, to our own devices and, of course, got up to mischief. Once, having watched *William*

Tell on our small black-and-white television, my brother decided to re-enact it. He made himself a bow and arrow – a nice sharp pointed arrow – and cajoled, threatened or bribed me to stand at the bottom of the garden with an apple on my head. Fortunately for me, he was, and still is, a terrible shot.

I was nine and my brother fourteen when our sister Nina was born. She was a surprising, lovely addition to our family. Looking back, I think I was a little jealous and resentful at the time, as until then I was the darling baby girl of the family. While my mother went back to work, my sister was looked after by an old lady in our street. We called her 'Nanny', and she looked like one. She had grey hair pulled together in a bun, and always seemed to have an apron on and a broom in her hand. I know that she loved my sister and regarded her as her own.

As both our parents worked we all had to help and work together. Life settled into a routine. On Thursday night we would meet our mother at the bus stop and go to the supermarket for the weekly shop. Before shopping night, I would sometimes sit with my mother writing out the weekly shopping list. We would write next to the items how much they would cost and see if we had enough money to buy all the groceries we needed. I remember one time being short of just a few pennies, so we adjusted the list so that it matched the money.

Friday was cleaning night and Saturday morning our washing day. I would walk to the laundrette with the weekly wash in a shopping trolley. I used to love this job as it was warm there and I could take time out to read my favourite book without being disturbed.

One job that gave me nightmares was the weekly dusting of our official Front Room. My mother loved ornaments and the room was full of them, from little porcelain birds, to large vases with artificial flowers; something on every level – and there were lots of levels. Each ornament would remind her of some situation or person. I can hear you asking, 'So where's the problem? Why the nightmares?' Well, I was not the most careful of girls; I never walked if I could run and, to put it bluntly, I was clumsy. Each Friday I would stop at the doorway, take a deep breath, and hope that this week would go by without me breaking anything.

My mother would complain to my father as, week by week, the official Front Room became sparser and sparser. But he would just say that I had to learn as one day I would have a home of my own. Sunday was a day of rest, although my mother still worked, knitting or making dresses for us, while she watched her favourite old black-and-white films – especially the musicals – on television.

Often, I would not see my father for days because of his shifts. If he were on a late shift, I would be in bed when he came home, and he would be asleep when I got up for school. When he was on an early shift, he would go to bed early, often after dinner. He liked working weekends as he was paid time-and-a-half, or double-time, and the money was needed. During the school holidays, I would see him more. I remember him preparing his sandwiches for work the next day, buttering the bread and putting on whatever filling was at hand. He also had a tin container for his hot drinks. He worked hard for us and he was often tired, but I never heard him grumble or complain. He used to say that his job was to go to work and our job was to go to school. He was a good, loving father and I knew that he loved us all. But I do regret that circumstances meant that I could not spend much time with him.

The weekly ordering of our lives, the budgeting, the discipline and the working together were all essential life lessons. These lessons came in very useful when I got married and had a family, and I am so grateful for them. I have to admit that, at the time, I did my fair share of complaining and moaning as I wanted to be out with my friends, not indoors learning these life lessons!

While my parents were Greek Orthodox, we did not attend the church regularly. We would go at Easter and Christmas, but I knew my parents' faith was there. In the alcove of our hall, my father had a shrine-like setup, where he had pictures of the saints, of Jesus, and a cross, separated by a net curtain across the area. Each night before going to bed, he would lift the curtain and pray.

I became what was called in those days a 'latchkey kid'. Even from the young age of nine or ten, I remember coming home with my own key; in winter, putting the paraffin heater on, preparing my own snack, and waiting till my parents came back. If I was sick, my mother still had to go to work, and I would often be left at home on my own. When I was in trouble, and my parents were at work, only I could sort myself out. This helped me to become strong, independent and resourceful.

Sometimes I would arrive home from school and realise that I had left my key at home. No one else would be home for at least another two hours, so I had to either sit on the doorstep waiting, or work out a plan. Never one to shirk a challenge, I came up with an idea. I would go next door and knock, and ask if I could go through their house, and climb over their garden fence into our garden. Undaunted, I would see if any window was open, so I could pull myself in. The top section of the lounge window had two narrow louvres of glass that were often open. I would slide the panes of glass out, one by one, and lay them on the ground. I could then stand on the windowsill – I was small in those days – pull myself up, and crawl through the small open space, falling onto the couch underneath. Sometimes the lounge window would be closed, so I would climb up to the flat roof of our kitchen extension and repeat the process through the bathroom window – but this time there was no couch to break my fall!

Looking back, it was that independence, that strength, that resourcefulness, that saw us through when our lives later took a violent, unexpected turn, and I so appreciate it now. But at the time I felt hard done by, and was often resentful that my mother had to work. I know that my parents had to work hard for us to survive, but I think we all missed out, not having more time together.

Despite these positive effects, I remember growing up having little sense of self-confidence or self-worth. Whether the early events of my childhood birthed those feelings in me, or whether it was just growing up, I accepted those negative thoughts too. Some of those feelings may have been generational, an independent and self-reliant front to mask my feelings of insecurity, caused by the belief that there was no one there for me. I know now that there were myriad reasons why I had these negative views of myself, and the Lord has been healing me extensively in this area. At the time, however, I brought these emotions with me, into all my relationships – especially with John – causing problems between us.

Life was not all work and no play; I remember so many times of laughter, song and dance. My mother loved to sing and dance, and I am sure my love of dancing comes from her.

We had a party for my sister's christening. It seemed that the whole house was full of people. And the food! The stuffed vine leaves, glistening with rich olive oil, koftas, fried to perfection, the crisp, fresh coriander salad that no Greek meal is without, and the rich, slow-cooked lamb – I can almost smell the food now as I write; it was heaven on a plate. The music, the song and the dancing seemed to go on forever.

On another occasion, I came down one morning after a party the night before, and saw what I thought was a glass of water. I took a gulp and realised that it was Ouzo which I quickly spat out.

Easter was a huge celebration in our family, with church, friends and lots of food – especially the kebabs my father would cook in our garden. He would be out there, in his shorts and white vest, with a cigarette in his hand, as he fanned the coals to get the heat just right to cook the lamb. After dinner, my mother would sing all the Greek songs from back home, and even my brother would join in – a taste of Cyprus in north London.

My favourite time was Christmas. The Christmas tree – we always had a huge one – would be put up in the bay window in the official Front Room, and we would all decorate it. Then the television was moved into the Front Room and over the Christmas period we were allowed to be in there. Christmas was also the time I would have a new dress to wear. I loved just lying there in the dark with only the Christmas lights on. Friends would come around, on Christmas night or Boxing night, and we would all eat leftovers, play cards and, of course, sing.

When I was seven or eight, I remember looking out my

window and seeing a girl walking down the street. She was wearing a bright green uniform. I did not know the girl; all I knew was that I wanted that uniform. Somehow we found out that she belonged to a Christian organisation called Campaigners, similar to Guides. They met at the Evangelical church around the corner from us every Thursday after school. I wanted to go and I remember the discussion I had with my mother about it, which went something like this:

'Mum, I want to go to Campaigners.'

'But you can't.'

'Why not?'

'Because you have just started your ballet and tap classes.'

'I want to go.'

'But you are doing so well, look at the shows you have been in. You love your dancing.'

'I want to go.'

'But I have just spent all this money on your shoes and costumes.'

'I want to go.'

This went on for a while, until I finally wore my poor mother down, and she finally gave in. As you can see, from a very young age I was a very determined girl. I just wanted to wear the bright green uniform.

I joined Campaigners, and part of being a Campaigner was attending church every Sunday. Although as a family we were Greek Orthodox, my parents were happy for me to attend the local Evangelical church and to join Campaigners. I think their view was that it was better to be in any church than to be playing on the streets.

I loved attending the church and did so for the next thirteen years. It was so different from Greek Orthodox churches, with all their icons, paintings, rituals, priests and incense. Even at that young age, I instinctively rejected all that, so when I walked into that bare, local church hall it felt so right. I loved the people, I loved hearing about the Lord, and the church became my second home. I would go to summer camps with Campaigners, learn more about Jesus and, at each camp, give my heart to Him again. I thank God that He arranged for the girl to walk outside my window, just as I was watching. I often speculate as to where I might be if I had not seen that bright green uniform.

When I was sixteen I left school to pursue a career in flower arranging, but changed my mind and after six weeks went back to school to do my 'A' levels. We were in a separate block, called the Sixth Form, where all the streams were together. There I noticed a handsome boy called John Helvadjian. In fact, we had been in the same school for years but had never met because we were in different streams. He had long hair, wore a long afghan coat and drove a gold Ford Capri. Not only was he dishy, but all the girls were vying for his attention. Well, as I said, I'm always up for a challenge, and I set myself the task of getting him to ask me out.

My mother reminded me that I would say to her, on numerous occasions, 'I'm going to get him.' We were in the same social group at school and at social events, but he was always aloof. I know now that he was shy. Eventually, I wore him down and we went out a few times but, to be honest, the chase was more interesting than the catch. I found him boring and not much fun. Meanwhile, John began to date my girlfriend, Sally.

One evening, Sally and I, and some of our group, went to one of the guys' house to listen to the new musical *Jesus Christ Superstar*. Sally was a Christian and had prayed beforehand that someone would become a Christian that night through listening to the music. Little did she know it would be me.

In the room, with the music playing in the background, people were chatting and messing about, but I was following the lyrics. I cannot remember which song it was, but the lyrics spoke to me like nothing else had previously. They spoke about the reason for Jesus dying, and how He suffered, and it just broke me. I looked around; everyone else was chatting and I could feel the tears welling up. I rushed out of the room to the only place I could be alone – the toilet (yes, I know, but it was a large toilet). I knelt down on my knees and, suddenly, it was as if a door between my head and my heart had opened, and all that I had learned sunk deep into my heart. I realised that, until then, I had made only a mental assent to Jesus, but this time it was for real.

I sobbed my heart out as I realised the enormity of His sacrifice for me and His love. I repented before the Lord and asked Him to come into my life and be Lord and Saviour. I don't know how long I was there, but when I came out I was completely different. I had a lightness in my heart and a joy which I had never experienced before. When I went back to join the others, I tried to tell them I had become a Christian, but they ignored me and said, 'You have always been a Christian.' I wanted to explain the difference – previously it was religion and self-righteousness that I spoke out of – but now it was for real. I had a relationship with the Lord, not a religion. They just shrugged their shoulders.

In 1972, when I turned eighteen, I left home and went to live in Earl's Court while training to be a hotel housekeeper with the Grand Metropolitan Hotels. I planned to train and then work on cruise liners, preferably one going to Australia. To this day, I do not know why Australia.

About a month after I started, John and a couple of other

friends turned up and we went out for the evening. I was going out with a Christian guy called Tom, whom I thought I was madly in love with, so did not give John a second look, or thought. He was just a friend, but he told me that Sally had finished with him because he was not a Christian.

A couple of days later, John called and said that he would like to take me out. So we went out a few times, just as friends. Even though he was not a Christian, I liked him a lot. This time he was definitely not boring and was even more handsome than I remembered. So I finished my relationship with Tom and started seriously going out with John.

I ignored the niggling thought that John was not a Christian; I was having too much of a good time. But the Lord loved me too much to let me go on my merry way for too long. On my training course I had befriended another Christian girl (I cannot remember her name), who lived in the same hostel as I did. I was not listening to the Lord so He used another tactic; He used this Christian friend. One day she asked me into her room and quietly confronted me with the truth. She said that it was not right to go out with a non-Christian and quoted me 2 Corinthians 6:14–15, verses that spoke about how we should not be yoked with an unbeliever. I just stared at her, not knowing what to say. We were not that close so it must have taken some courage on her part to confront me. I think I just stammered, 'Thank you for telling me,' and then left.

I wasn't thankful for what she had told me because I had to do something about it now I had been confronted with the truth. It was a lot easier when I had buried it. It was a difficult time; my emotions were all over the place. John was very dishy, charming and I *really, really* liked him. He had met my family; my parents loved him and used to call him

'John the Baptist' because of his long hair and afghan coat. It was then that John found out that I was called Rita, and decided to ditch the name Barbara – I would be known as Rita from then on. He was becoming part of us, part of me. I wrestled with it for that whole day. My thoughts were all over the place from, 'Yes, I will finish with him,' to 'Well, maybe God brought him to me so that he would come to the Lord.' Maybe this 'word' from my friend was not from God but from the enemy, to stop John from coming to the Lord. After all, doesn't the enemy use scripture as well? Finally, I was confronted by the question: 'Who do I love more, the Lord or John?' I knew, however hard it was, that there was no contest – I chose the Lord. I decided that when I saw John that evening I would finish our relationship. I would tell him why, and then let him go.

That night, when I opened the door to John at the hostel, I saw a smiling, beaming John who could not keep still. He was bouncing up and down on the steps mumbling something like, 'I did it! I did it!'

'What have you done?' I said, having no clue as to what he was on about. It was as if he was 'high' on something. John just kept repeating, 'I did it!' Men were not allowed to come into the hostel, so we stood on the steps to talk. Finally, I managed to get some sense out of him. When he told me what he had done, I was utterly speechless for once. He had given his heart to the Lord, on the very day I was wrestling with what to do, the day I decided to finish our relationship. It was as if God was giving His approval for us to be together. From that moment on our relationship went from strength to strength.

CHAPTER THREE

MARRIED LIFE AND SPIRITUAL BATTLES

Rita and *John*

It was a cold but sunny day on 12th October 1974 when we got married. Since I wanted to walk down the aisle and our church was a modern building with no aisle, we got married in an old Anglican church in Southgate, north London. It was a small wedding but with a full choir. Most of the guests (apart from shivering) were wondering whether this marriage would survive as we were so young – we were both twenty years old. We were oblivious to this, of course, caught up in the excitement and romance of the day.

The wedding was held at 12.00 p.m. so that photos could be taken while it was still light, and was followed by an afternoon reception at a local hotel. Since I loved dancing, a disco was held after the wedding lunch, even though it was still afternoon. We left for our honeymoon at 6.00 p.m. and travelled that same day to Norfolk where we had rented a cottage. We were both happy, the day had gone so well, and we were looking forward to our life ahead.

However, the journey to our wedding day had not gone so well. The issue of my ethnicity had arisen.

Generally, with previous girlfriends, I had been reluctant to take them home to introduce them to the rest of my family. Deep down, I knew that my mum wanted me to be interested in Armenian girls and ultimately to marry one. As her only son, she wanted me to keep both the Armenian pedigree and the Helvadjian name undefiled. When Mum noticed that I was getting serious with Rita, she asked me why I could not 'choose' an Armenian girl, as she knew many of them. I ignored my parents. It was my life, and I was going to do what mattered to me, not what suited them.

In April 1974 I decided that it was the right time to move the relationship on. Being a romantic, I proposed to Rita while she was doing the ironing.

'Do you fancy a long engagement or a short one?' I asked.

'Short one,' she replied, without missing a crease, and the deed was done.

So the following Saturday we went to the local jewellers near where Rita lived and bought the ring. When we returned home, Rita's mother was painting the skirting board, and we duly informed her that we were engaged. Rita's parents were happy. They had already anticipated this would happen and we all celebrated.

Then I had to tell my parents that Rita and I were engaged. I was met with a frosty response. I was only twenty years old and, as I was so young, they hoped this engagement idea would fizzle out. However, we had started making arrangements for the wedding and, at some point, both sets of parents would have to meet. Deep down, I dreaded this moment. I knew that, even though Rita's father had converted from the Muslim faith and was now a Christian, the only thing that would register with my parents was that he was Turkish and that their future daughter-in-law was half-Turkish and half-Greek.

The day came and the parents met; it transpired that my father knew Rita's dad from Cyprus, and he registered that his son was marrying not only someone who was not Armenian, but also a girl who was half-Turkish. After the meeting, my mother cried and asked me, 'Why are you doing this?' The atmosphere at home became tense, as did my relationship with my parents. In hindsight I could have handled the whole process better; I could have taken the time to listen to my parents' point of view and tried to understand where they were coming from. Although I knew about the massacre of the Armenians by the Turks, I did not fully understand the impact that the stories of the past behaviour of the Turks had had on my parents. I could have taken the time to listen, even though it would not have changed my mind about marrying Rita. I could at least have discussed it with them, instead of just telling them that it was my life, and that was that. Also, I could not see what the past events had to do with me now. All I wanted to do was to get married and leave home, so I paid little attention to what my parents were thinking or going through. My parents' reaction to Rita erected a barrier in my relationship with them and, as a result, I left them out of most of the wedding arrangements.

For me, it was a bewildering time. I could not understand why I was being rejected for something past generations of mine might have done. I had grown up with the story of my father's conversion, along with his comments that Turks could not be trusted. As far as I was concerned, I was as much a victim of the Turks as John's parents were. After all, we were all Christians. I was nineteen years old, lacking self-confidence and self-worth and this rejection reinforced negative views I had about myself. There were times when I would go round to John's house and the atmosphere would be tense, making me feel very vulnerable. Often this was not due to me but because of the strained relationship between John and his parents. However, I felt very insecure and uncomfortable on those visits.

In some situations John was torn between his parents and me, which added to my insecurity. For example, on one occasion I went round to John's house to find his parents very angry at me because of the wedding invitations. I had followed the English custom of the bride's parents being the hosts and inviting the guests, and John's parents were not happy that they were not included in this. I took the full force of their anger, as they confronted me about the invitations, even though the decision had been made in agreement with John. Their rejection of me, my feelings of not being good enough, and anger at the way they perceived my parents all caused me to explode. I shouted at them, 'And you are meant to be Christians!' John was there but did not intervene. I was so angry; I threw the ring at him and ran out of the house. He neither followed me nor contacted me until much later.

He had stayed to sort things out with his parents, which may have been commendable but it caused me further problems. I felt I was less important to him than his parents were, and that he was putting them first, just when I needed his support. I felt like an outsider and I became even more insecure. Though we subsequently made it up, it didn't help, and it was only later on when we began our journey of personal prayer ministry that these events came to the fore, needing healing and forgiveness. Only then, did I finally accept my ethnicity.

John's parents were godly people who loved their son, and so gradually they came to accept the situation. But there was a tacit understanding that my true ethnicity would be hidden from their extended families, especially the two grandmothers who had gone through so much at the hands of the Turks. They were all told that I was of Greek parentage and, even to this day, still don't know. To protect my parents, I didn't tell them any of this.

Meanwhile, we had decided that we would not get married until we were able to buy our own home. John had managed to save regularly in a building society, and had enough for a deposit on a small flat located further north of where we were living. During this search, John's parents lovingly and generously gave us a gift of £3,000 so that we could buy a property. We were able to stretch ourselves and, with their gift, purchased instead a three-bedroom semi-detached house in a better area. We were now settled, though mortgaged to the hilt, and we set a date for the wedding.

When we returned from our honeymoon, we began the process of the two-becoming-one married life. We were young and in love so the physical becoming-one was easy. However, the practical working-out of becoming-one was a different story. Each of us brought into the marriage our own baggage and our own issues. I brought my insecurities, lack of self-confidence, lack of self-worth and an idealistic view of how the man should act (I had been reading too many Mills & Boon romance novels). My view of how a man should be put unrealistic expectations and pressures on John to behave in a certain way. If he did not, then I would react, making sure he knew of my disapproval. I would either withdraw or make pointed remarks about how one of my girlfriend's partner's had brought them flowers, or spoiled them. John then felt inadequate and would react by doing the exact opposite to what I wanted, causing me to complain about him even more. At the same time, I was very afraid of losing him and needed constant reassurance.

I came into the marriage with my own fears and insecurities, which I hid by being arrogant and aloof. I couldn't discuss these issues and would become defensive if criticised. If I wasn't happy with Rita, I would just withdraw emotionally, which made her both shaky and fearful, and reinforced her poor view of herself. Often she would just give in, to stop me withdrawing. I also came to the marriage with a phobia of blood, sickness and hospitals. I couldn't discuss operations or illness. Even today, we are not sure where the root of this fear comes from, but we could see the fruit of it. One thing that I had been doing, which we discovered fuelled this fear, was reading books on the Third Reich. All the material and the pictures of the genocide of the Jews made the fears worse and, for the first six months of marriage, I couldn't eat meat or even look at it. I couldn't walk past a butcher's window without it affecting me. Perhaps we should have done something about this, but we just thought that it was a phase and that everybody has some phobias.

We were like two tectonic plates, moving around each other and occasionally clashing, causing an earthquake. In the first couple of years, there were many 'earthquakes'; some low on the Richter Scale, others on the high side. In my frustration and anger, I would storm out of the house; John, very occasionally, would do so too. So we decided that storming out had to stop. We made a rule that, from then on, if one of us stormed out of the house, then the marriage was over. Occasionally I marched to the front door and grabbed the handle. Then I would remember the agreement and slowly turn back. We were also individuals with different interests. I loved dancing, John did not; I loved reading, John did not; I loved parties, John did not, and so on. On John's side, I did not like football, rugby, athletics – any sport really – history, beer, and so on. If we needed any evidence that the Lord had a sense of humour, we only had to look at ourselves.

Despite our issues and differences, we were happy and glad to be together. There were more fun times than sad times. We looked forward to the future together and were just like any other couple.

I was now commuting into the city and John worked with his father in his uncle's business. We did not have much money; we had scrimped and saved just to manage to buy the house, so there was no money left over for furniture or heating. The house was old with only an antique coal-fired boiler in the kitchen to heat water. John's parents, pitying us, paid for central heating to be installed – a lifesaver. John's old single bed became our couch in the lounge, and we had an old black-and-white television, donated by his grandma, and my brother's old double bed – we were set. There were roughly set old curtains that barely covered the windows. From the outside the house looked as if squatters were living there.

Often, Sally (yes, John's old girlfriend, who was also one of my bridesmaids) came around with her boyfriend, Peter, who was a professional golfer. He and John would go off to the driving range while Sally and I would have a natter. Once when they came around, I noticed straightaway that something was different about Sally. As soon as the men left, I rounded on her: 'What's happened to you? You look so different. Come on, spill the beans!'

Sally told me that she and Peter had started going to a small group, where they had been taught about the baptism of the Holy Spirit and speaking in tongues. This was all new to me. The church I had grown up in had never spoken of the Holy Spirit in such a way, or referred to the gifts of the Spirit. I could see the difference in her and wanted to have what she had. So I asked her to pray for me, for the baptism of the Spirit, right there. Sally was a little taken aback, it was probably her first time praying for others, but she laid hands on me and prayed. Immediately I felt the presence of the Holy Spirit and spoke in tongues. It transported me to another dimension, and was the missing part of my walk with the Lord.

It caused problems between us, because suddenly Rita was not on the same level as me. She was babbling in an unknown tongue, her prayer life was different, and she was different. She was not the woman I signed up for. As Rita wanted more of the Holy Spirit, she wanted to go to the house group that Sally and Peter were going to. In fact, the meeting was held a couple of streets from where my parents lived. So in February 1975 we began to attend. After about a month or so, I could not deny what I saw, or the teaching about the Holy Spirit, and I too asked for the baptism of the Holy Spirit.

This was a significant event in our spiritual lives. It opened up another world for us and led us into a deeper walk with the Lord. It brought us into fellowship with others who believed that what happened in the book of the Acts of the Apostles in the Bible was happening now in the twentieth century. We were exposed to healings, deliverance and the power of prayer. This foundational teaching became important in our lives both for our own personal walk and, later, as we walked into prayer ministry.

As the house group grew we decided to meet once a week in a school hall, as a whole body, and in cell groups mid-week. It was such a blessing for us to be part of Frank and Betty's cell group. They were a lovely couple, now with the Lord, about twenty years older than us. The four of us became good friends but, most of all, they became spiritual parents to us, a relationship which persisted, in some form or another, for over thirty years.

Frank was a practical joker, full of fun, and we have many happy memories of our time with them. We introduced them to garlic, pizzas and Greek food. They introduced us to half a pint of lager and lime (of course not too strong!). One summer, it seemed, we spent going around trying different pub gardens enjoying a glass of our favourite tipple – lager and lime – along with hilarious conversation.

But Frank taught us about being hungry for God, studying His word, and personal spiritual development. When I started having spiritual problems, it was to Frank and Betty that we turned.

It was around early 1976 when I began to suffer in my mind. Whenever I tried to sleep, pressure or a block would appear in my mind and stop me from sleeping. Standing on the platform at the station, I would hear voices telling me to jump in front of the train. Sometimes the voices would be so bad that I would have to grip the post on the platform. I could not get any mental rest.

One night it was very bad and I was praying for Rita as she wrestled with the whole situation. As I prayed, I could see what looked like two horns on her head. I prayed further and saw something leave Rita. I opened the window and watched it go out of the room. By now it was midnight and I was feeling shaken and entirely out of my depth. Despite the time, I called Frank and Betty for help, and they said to come round immediately.

We are made up of three parts: mind, body and spirit. We were created for our spiritual part to be fulfilled by the Holy

Spirit, to enable us to have a relationship with Father God. People either suppress their spirituality or seek some ways to fulfil it. Today we see a resurgence of people seeking ways to express their spirituality, often in the New Age movement or Eastern religions. I had grown up in a church in which the things of the Spirit were not taught, or in any way expressed. As a teenager, I had a keen spiritual awareness, which was not being fulfilled or expressed in my walk with the Lord as it should have been. Instead it was channelled into the wrong spiritual direction. I became involved in the occult: holding séances in my home with friends, where I acted as the medium, opening myself up to all things demonic. I became involved in levitation, meditation, the reading of horoscopes, and trying to know the future by the reading of coffee dregs (a Greek custom). I did not do this very often, but it was enough; I was only around fourteen at that time, and was ignorant of what I was really getting myself into. I did not receive any teaching about the Holy Spirit, demons or the ways of the devil. However, ignorance does not protect one from the consequences of one's actions.

In Frank's study that night, after a few discerning questions unfolding these past events, he taught us about the dangers of the occult, how demons operate, and the consequences of sin. After I repented, I was both delivered and healed. This was another important event in our spiritual life. Not only was I at peace but we had a first-hand experience of the spiritual world. Little did we know, at that time, that this was one of the Lord's teaching sessions, preparing us for our future ministry. But, more importantly, it was the first of many such experiences that the Lord would take us through.

We had decided that we would not have children, but intended to set ourselves up and then go travelling. Our lives would be all about us – we are so grateful that instead I became broody. Today, with two children and six grandchildren, we can't believe that we so nearly missed out on all these blessings. In 1977 I fell pregnant, and we were both very happy.

However, when Rita was just three months pregnant, my father and I were made redundant because my uncle had sold the company. At that time, Rita earned more than I did and the mortgage was paid from her monthly wage. There was very little left over for anything else. We were still building-up our house; the kitchen and bathroom were original. And now in four months, Rita would be leaving work to have our first child. It was a dark time, with many uncertainties ahead of us. I struggled and became depressed when I couldn't get a job. When my redundancy money ran out, I had to claim unemployment benefit. I thought this shameful and became more depressed, but I had no choice; we needed the money. All of God's children, at some time, have to go through a time of testing and trusting the Lord. The lessons learned by Rita helping her mother to budget now became invaluable. We managed but, looking back, we are not sure how. Meanwhile, my father and I decided to set up our own business with my brother-in-law. By early December, a week before Rita was due to stop work, the company started; it was all very close.

Mark Andrew Helvadjian arrived at 9.00 p.m. on 8th February 1978. As he was late, Rita had to be induced and the labour lasted the whole day. At that time, it was fashionable and expected for the father to be present at the birth, both to help the father to bond with the child and to support the mother. We went along with that expectation, forgetting to take into consideration my aversion to blood, sickness and hospitals. We did not realise how deep the aversion was, or that its root lay in my fear of death. For the whole day, I was in the one place I dreaded – a hospital – confronted by blood, medical procedures, and gore: all the things I was afraid of. For me, they all represented death; I could not see how life could be a part of them. Rita was linked to all the things I feared, and now another layer of fear was added – the fear of her dying. The whole experience proved to be extremely traumatic for me.

Having not experienced anything like this before, I went on to bury the day's events and the emotions attached to them. The only way I could do this was to shut myself off. As Rita was part of the trauma, I also withdrew from her. Shutting things out was the way I had coped in the past, and this event was no different. It was a conflicting time for me; on the one hand I was over the moon having Mark, and so proud of him, but on the other hand, I was struggling to keep it all together.

I could sense John was withdrawing and I was bewildered. He was so proud of Mark and loved him, he continually hugged him and told him that he loved him, but why was he withdrawing from me? The business was still new, and John was working almost 24/7 to make it a success. I was busy with Mark, so there was no time to reflect, or to deal with the issues that the birth had raised. We just buried them and got on with the cycle of life. Anyway, there were more important challenges ahead, such as paying the bills and being parents for the first time, and John's withdrawal from me only lasted a short time.

However, it was a mistake on our part not to try to address these issues, with help, and learn from them. We now understand that traumatic and negative events in one's life do not just go away because we bury them. Traumatic events can lay dormant, deep within our subconscious, and accumulate over time until they unexpectedly erupt, like a volcano. John's fear of death and of losing me was not resolved; it sank deep within him, only to surface much later.

We decided that we would like two children, as close together as possible, so that they would be friends as well as siblings. I thought that, if I was going to be home with one child, I might as well be with two. So I fell pregnant again in 1978, and the baby was due in 1979 – only sixteen and a half months between the children – just as we wanted. We both wanted John to be at the birth again, the trauma that he experienced the first time was long forgotten, not even a whisper of memory came to us. John did not want to miss his second child's arrival, but the situation was taken out of his control by the business; he had to leave just before David John Helvadjian arrived, on 28th June 1979.

We were overjoyed. We had our two wonderful sons, a lovely home, a business that was growing and life was good. We were complete, or so we thought, but the Lord had other plans. In 1983 I discovered I was pregnant for a third time, which disrupted our plans and our comfortable way of life.

CHAPTER FOUR

THE POWER OF THE WORD

Rita and *John*

In January 1983, an unexpected pregnancy was a shock, totally unplanned. We did not see it as a blessing or a gift from the Lord, rather a rude disruption to our cosy, well-planned life. We were delighted with our lot and did not see the need to add anything further to it. Our boys were aged only four and three, and we thought having another child so soon would cause problems. Suddenly we needed to think about bigger cars, a bigger house, requiring more money and, of course, more nappies.

In retrospect, there should have been no issues about having a third child. We were a healthy, loving family and we could have worked it out. But at the time we struggled with the thought of having another child.

The situation was compounded by the fact that I fell pregnant even though I was using an IUD, which caused problems within the pregnancy. The doctors told me that if I were able to carry the baby until the sixteenth week, then it would be fine. I felt sick all the time and had to spend a fair bit of time in bed. John was busy with the business so most of the time I struggled to cope on my own.

But the biggest issue was John's reaction to this baby. It was as if a switch had flicked in him, and he went from being his usual self to a shadow of himself, both physically and emotionally. He hardly ate, had trouble sleeping and, once again, withdrew emotionally and physically from me. I was still insecure and dependent on him. If he was fine, I was too; if he was not, neither was I. John's strong adverse reaction to the baby and the effect it had on our relationship, led me to view this baby even more as causing trouble. It seemed to me that John had withdrawn because he blamed me for the pregnancy. I couldn't understand what was happening, or why another baby would cause him to act the way he was, especially since he had never reacted like this when I was pregnant with Mark or David.

I couldn't understand it either. Why should Rita being pregnant cause me such inner distress? What trigger had made me become so depressed and withdrawn from Rita? To this day, reflecting on the past, it is unclear what was going on in my subconscious. Could it have been that I wrongly connected pregnancy with death, or was it a fear that something would happen to Rita? Perhaps in my mind, life, death, sickness and hospitals were all mixed up together. I was not able to separate them or rationalise the differences between them. Whatever the cause, my severe reaction was a form of self-preservation: I could not cope with reality.

I would try to maintain normality for the boys and pretend to friends and family that all was well, but the stress, pressure and worry were affecting me. When I asked John what the matter was he would reply, 'Nothing', making me feel as if I had imagined things. I knew I did not imagine the strained atmosphere between us, or John's withdrawal, and I knew there was something wrong with him. Once again, John's inability to discuss or confront issues caused me to be both frustrated and afraid. I would often erupt, and we had frequent arguments in the evenings. On a couple of occasions, John stormed out and drove away – our previous agreement was forgotten. Later I found out that it was in those times that John was fighting the voices in his head which were urging him to drive the car into a brick wall and kill himself. One evening, I'd had enough and shouted at him in tears, 'Go on, get out. I'll look after all three of us,' as I swung open the lounge door for him to leave.

This hit me like a bucket of cold water. I suddenly woke up and, as Rita spoke to me, I promised to see Frank and talk about what was going on. We thank God for Frank, for his time and his wisdom. We did not discuss what had happened; I was unwilling – nor did Rita question me. She was just thankful that things had settled back into normality. Looking back, we are again aware of how many things we just buried because we could not face the reality of what we were going through at the time. And we are sure that we were not the only couple who lived like that.

I was now in my fourteenth week and the baby was fine. John was emotionally and physically 'back' with me. Together we had accepted the baby and were looking forward to its arrival. We spoke about names, what sex we thought the baby would be, and began to make plans for the future with another lovely addition to our family.

One Saturday night, my mother came to babysit and we went out for a meal just to enjoy being together on our own. It was a special time of sharing, chatting and being excited about the future. All seemed well, and the baby seemed to be growing fine in the comfort of my womb.

But that night I was woken up by her waters breaking, and the baby was born at home. It was the sixteenth week;

the doctors told me it was not a miscarriage but a mini labour. No baby can survive being born at sixteen weeks. John called my parents to look after the boys, then he called the doctor who, in turn, immediately called the ambulance.

We sensed in our spirits that it was a girl and we were going to call her Rea. She would have been born in September 1983. For many, many years, around September time, we would think about her with sadness. We would try to imagine what she would have been like, her character, her personality, and we would count the number of years as she got older. We know we will see her again one day.

Just when we had begun to accept and love her, she was taken from us. We were in shock. We could not understand what was happening or why. The whole four months, it seemed like we were living in a dream, and now we had woken up. We could not understand any of it, especially John's behaviour. We missed the correlation between his withdrawal this time, and at Mark's birth. For us, they were two separate incidents. It was only later, when events further unfolded, that we understood that this was another layer of pressure building up in his mind.

A few days after I came out of hospital, we were confronted by some devastating news. We were told that John's mother had an advanced type of bone cancer. A few months previously, she had undergone the traumatic experience of having a mastectomy and, after the operation, the doctor had reassured her that they had removed all traces of cancer; that she was now all clear and could look forward to her recovery. When she complained about having pains in her shoulder and back, she was reassured that they were unrelated and she was free of cancer. However, by April the pain was so bad that she went for further consultation. The first doctor had gotten it wrong; the cancer was now well advanced, and had spread to her bones.

Our attention was focused on supporting John's mother and father. Any opportunity was lost for us to talk about our baby, make some sense of what happened, and grieve. We just pushed the whole matter down, into the basement of our subconscious, and soldiered on. We were attending a small house group that Frank and Betty had started with a few people. Our Christian circle was very small; no one thought of praying for healing for us, or of helping us to deal with the trauma of the death of our baby. It seemed in those days that one was just expected to get on with life.

John's parents attended the local Baptist church where we lived, and had informed the minister about his mother's sickness and the loss of our baby. The minister contacted us to make a time for a visit. When he came, he was very compassionate and spent time talking to us but, again, there was no focus on inner healing. He just finished the visit with a covering prayer. It was only later on in our spiritual walk that we learned the value of inner healing, prayer ministry, and the negative effect that grief, pain and trauma can have on a person. Later we also learned that the Greek word 'ozo', used in the New Testament for salvation, means saved, healed and whole. Jesus did not come just to save us and take us to heaven, but to heal and make us whole now, in this life. In our case, it would take another ten years before we dealt with our loss, pain, sin and grief.

It was a difficult time for us, especially for me. I was bitterly angry that the original doctors had misdiagnosed my mother's sickness entirely, and had reassured the family that the operation had been successful in removing all traces of cancer. I blamed them for getting it so wrong and causing evident distress to the family. My growing hatred of the medical profession further fuelled my phobia of doctors, surgeries and hospitals.

My younger sister, Hilda, was due to get married later that year, but the wedding was moved forward to July, on the doctors' advice. The wedding day was a joyous occasion, and Mum was well enough to enjoy the event and take part in the day as the bride's mother. But by the end of the year cancer had spread to her liver.

Meanwhile, we felt it was time to move house. Apart from being too small for us, we wanted a fresh new start. We wrote a list of qualities for our ideal house – even my wanting a magnolia tree in the front garden. We began looking and, by September, we had found the house. The Lord had given us everything on our list, even the magnolia tree in the garden. It was a lovely house, not too far from where we were. At the bottom of the road was a large, beautiful park with a lake in the middle. It was near to an idyllic village green and to schools. It was our blessed house. We moved in on our wedding anniversary, 12th October 1983, and it became our lovely family home until May 2006.

We entered 1984 with John's mum getting weaker. Hilda looked after her full-time while John's father still worked at the business.

I would go to visit, sometimes with the boys, at other times alone. It was during these visits that John's mum graciously asked me to forgive her and her husband for their actions at the beginning of my relationship with John. Of course, there was nothing left to forgive. Their actions and love showed that all the past prejudices had long gone, and I had nothing but love for them.

I found it very hard watching my mother getting frailer each day. I struggled to visit her, and the issues I still had with sickness and death made it worse. So I threw myself into the business, working hard, unwilling or unable to face the fact that my mother was deteriorating and dying.

In March 1984 the Lord took my mother home. Even though we knew that it would happen, it was still a shock to hear the news. Rita received the news with sadness and regret, but I had loved my mother dearly, and I was angry at God for taking her away, for the way she had died, slowly deteriorating over what seemed like an eternity, until at the end she was just skin and bone.

Two of the most stressful events in life are said to be bereavement and moving house. We had faced bereavement and moved house in one year, followed shortly, in the new year, by another death. We cannot say that we handled this all with wisdom or in a healthy way.

For us, the move was a blessed time, not at all stressful, and full of fun, especially when we tried to 'accidentally' leave our large white rabbit behind, as a gift for the new purchasers. The removers, thinking we had forgotten the rabbit, were kind-hearted enough to load him up with the rest of the furniture (hatch and poo included). The removal van turned up with the rabbit in the passenger seat beside the driver's mate. We tried to be thankful!

But the bereavements were a different matter. We never spent time dealing with or facing those heartaches. With the loss of our baby, there was no time. The ongoing cycle of life events took that out of our hands, even if we had known how to grieve the loss of our child. I dealt with the loss of my mother by shutting myself down and detaching from my emotions. I would not talk to anyone about how I was feeling, not even with Rita. I did not want any comfort or pity from anyone and, after a while, Rita just gave up. My default again was to get on with life and bury myself in my work.

We now often wonder if things would have been different if we'd had people around to minister to us at that time. Not just pray general prayers over us, but to allow us to express what we were feeling, to draw us out, to bring words of healing into our lives as Proverbs 12:18b NIV states, 'The tongue of the wise brings healing.' We are neither blaming nor judging the people around us. After all, we could have searched the scriptures and pressed into the Lord more, but we did not and have to take responsibility for our part. Perhaps what occurred subsequently with John's illness might have been averted, or lessened, had we acted differently.

In 1986 we had another addition to our family, this time of the four-legged variety. I had always wanted a dog and decided that the time was right to have one. Rita, on the other hand, was not too keen on the idea. When she was young her family had a few dogs as pets, but her experience was not a good one, especially with Blackie, a black Labrador that kept biting her ankles. I wanted a 'proper' dog to take out, befitting a real man, not one of those 'yappy' dogs which I called 'rats on leads'. Another important factor in my consideration was that the dog would protect Rita and the boys. Therefore it would have to be a brave, fierce dog, but good with children.

Once again, Frank came to the rescue with the perfect solution. He was enamoured with a breed of dog called Rhodesian Ridgebacks, and suggested they would be just ideal for the family. We looked-up the breed and were suitably impressed by their quality and temperament. Next we needed to find a breeder with a reputation for rearing a quality breed of Ridgebacks and we found just the right one in Manchester. The deal was done and, on 2nd January 1986, six-week-old Socs became the latest addition to our family. We named him Socs – short for Socrates, in line with the Greek side of Rita's ancestry – and also because he had white paws, just as though he was wearing white socks.

He was absolutely gorgeous. The whole family fell in love with him and, of course, despite being reluctant initially, I fell the hardest. He was a vital part of our family and so good with the boys. He would allow them to pull his ears, sit on his back and pretend he was a motorbike, where his ears doubled as handlebars. He was loyal, obedient (most of the time), and an appropriate dog for a man to take out. But he was not a guard dog. Granted, he looked fierce and a proper man's dog, but he was as 'yellow-belly' as custard. All the small, yappy dogs, which were a quarter of his size, would just bark at him and Socs would run away. Even the local cats found out about his inability to uphold the integrity of his kind and would run rings around him. Much laughter was had at John's expense about Socs, the ferocious 'guard dog'.

After a few years of meeting regularly in a house group with Frank and Betty we felt it was time to move. We thought a larger body of believers would be better for us as a family, especially so the boys would have Christian friends. In late 1986 we moved to the local Baptist church. It was a lovely spiritual home for us; it was not 'charismatic' as we were used to, no speaking in tongues or any visible workings of the Spirit, but it was there that we learned about living in community. The teaching was solid, the children's church was good, and we all felt very much at home.

We were very content; we had a new home, a new spiritual home and of course our wonderful 'guard dog' Socs. We were blessed.

All went well until around 1988 when trouble flared up again in my mind. I was tormented and could not find any mental rest. One day I was walking the dog in the park when I cried out to the Lord, 'If you don't do something, I'll end up in a mental home.'

Then almost immediately, Gill came to my mind. A few months before, I had started a prayer group for the mums at school and Gill was a part of the group. I had noticed that she was slightly different; her prayers were more powerful and direct; she had a firm belief that God healed, and she had herself been physically and miraculously healed by the Lord. I also remembered that Gill had mentioned that she and her husband were involved in an organisation called Wholeness Through Christ. Straight away I went home, ditched Socs, and rushed around to Gill's house.

Gill must have been surprised when I suddenly turned up on her doorstep. She listened as I blurted out all that I was going through: the mental torment and pressure in my mind, the feeling of panic and a constant heaviness. She must have realised the seriousness of my situation, and suggested that she and her husband Ben come round that evening to pray and talk with us.

That night Ben and Gill shared with us about spiritual principles, and the workings of the evil one in ways we had not heard before. Then they prayed for Rita. As Ben prayed for her, she slumped over, and he saw in the Spirit what resembled a black octopus on her back. Rita cannot recall the specific prayers that Ben prayed, but the only thing she knew was that something had shifted inside her and, as a result, she felt a sense of relief and peace in her mind.

That evening was a spiritual eye-opener for me and proved to be the start of a long journey of inner healing. In the following weeks, I went to see Gill for more prayer. It was a time of profound ministry for me, as the Lord revealed that I had held many wrong perceptions about Father God. Many were based on past negative experiences about the role of a father; some were my choosing to believe the lies of the enemy instead of the truth I read in the Bible. The Lord made me realise that I had grown up with a father who loved me, but was usually absent. God showed me that He was different; He healed me of past rejections, and gave me an understanding of my upbringing; He brought to mind many childhood experiences that had wounded me, and negative words spoken to me, and He healed them all.

I was delivered from the traps and snares of the enemy and more deliverance followed. But the enemy did not like the fact that I was, slowly and surely, being freed from him, and it was a battle.

One day, when I was driving to the school to collect the boys, I felt a physical presence of evil in the car; it felt like it was sitting between me and the steering wheel, pushing me to lose control. I cried out to the Lord, and started praising Him, declaring the blood of the Lamb over me. The blood of Jesus is the most potent thing on earth; the enemy cannot stand it and has to flee. I arrived at the school safe and sound.

While the whole process of healing was going on, I reflected on what was happening. The Lord reminded me of the parable of the two builders – the one who built his house on sand, and the other who built his house on rock (Matt. 7:24–27). He told me that He was moving the sand from underneath me, and replacing it with rock – Himself – so that when life's storms occurred, I would be able to stand and not fall.

There will always be storms in our lives, large or small, impacting us directly or indirectly. The Lord did say in John 16:33 that we will all have trouble in our lives. We are not immune from it but, when it happens, we are to take heart for He has overcome the world. The Lord's desire for us is to stand when these troubles come, not to fall over, and He has provided everything we need so that we can stand. This provision is available for all of us if we are willing to allow Him to change the foundation of our lives.

Rita always knew that what the Lord was doing in her life was out of love for her, but as she reflects on past events now, she also sees it as vital preparation for what was to come. When the 'storm' swirled into our lives later on, it was Rita who stood firm and steered us through that time. We dread to think what would have happened if both of us were based on shifting sand.

Our meeting up with Gill and Ben was life-transforming. It was as if we had been heading in one direction and then were suddenly pulled into another. As Rita became freer, our relationship with Gill and Ben developed and I grew interested as well. We had received the practical out workings of ministry through Gill and Ben but now we were interested in knowing how the ministry of Wholeness Through Christ operated.

Wholeness Through Christ held residential weeks away, called 'schools', where one was taught biblical principles, learned to minister, and be ministered to. You could attend one of these schools each year. After attending three schools, you might be invited to attend two further schools, which were for training to minister in Wholeness Through Christ.

We had absorbed all that Gill and Ben could show and teach us, but we wanted more. So we applied to go to one of the schools. Over the next three years we attended schools and were invited to attend the two further training schools.

These weeks away with Wholeness Through Christ were a revelation. We were taught about the effects of past generations on present generations, about blessings and curses (and cursed objects), the power of words, deliverance and how demons operate, bondages and the power of forgiveness. We learned how negative events in our lives could continue to cause problems in one's life if not healed. And we understood that the Lord wants us to be whole, that Jesus came to set us free, to heal us and to bring us peace. We saw the relevance of Isaiah 61:1–3, the very scriptures that Jesus used at the beginning of His ministry, in Luke 4:18–19. We realised that we could be free from our 'prisons', that we could be free from oppression, and that we did not have to be captives any longer to the works of the evil one.

All the teaching was biblically based, and we learned the power of the word. It was amazing to know, and see the sword of the Spirit, mentioned in Hebrews 4:12–13, used so effectively. The whole experience was very up-building, and enlarged our view of the Lord. The scriptures came alive in such a fresh new way.

Not only did we learn much attending the schools, but we received much. We attended them individually, so that one of us could be with the children, and that was very important. It meant that we could focus on ourselves without any distractions. It was a special time just for us. The Lord did deep work in each of us, which at times was painful but necessary to achieve full healing – just like when there is an infection in a wound, you have to make sure that it is all removed before you seal it up for healing.

During these weeks we saw and experienced the power of the Holy Spirit. Wholeness Through Christ based their ministry on Psalm 103:1–5, and we saw scripture being fulfilled in front of our own eyes, not just in others – but in our personal lives. We saw people being healed, set free, demons expelled from others, and from our own lives. Our faith grew by leaps and bounds.

But the most important thing those weeks did was to establish in us a foundation of God's love; our trust in Him increased, and gave us a firm belief that God can do anything. These foundational truths were vital later on, when we found ourselves confronted by our biggest challenge.

We used what we had been taught in our daily lives, praying intensely into situations around us, and for our children. Everything that the Lord set us free from we prayed for the children to be free from also. As we saw issues in our children, we would ask the Lord what the root was and how to pray. And we found ourselves ministering to others, as the Lord brought them to us.

We became part of the north London committee of Wholeness Through Christ, where we arranged and held Saturday Wholeness Through Christ days. Through this movement we met some wonderful people who taught us, and shared with us so many of God's truths. We did not realise at the time how important these people were and how much we would need them.

Being involved in Wholeness Through Christ transformed our lives. We do not believe we would be where we are today if it was not for their love, teaching and ministry. The teachings we learned at this time stood us in good stead for our future, and for our children, and for our children's children.

We had moved into a season of blessings and grace. We had moved on spiritually, we had a closer walk with the Lord and, while not all our issues were resolved, we were on the right road.

We became more involved in the church; both of us, at different times, became Deacons. I became a youth leader for the teenage group, as well as being part of the preaching team. Later on, as the church moved into healing, we were both part of the healing team. We ran a house group and assisted with 'Alpha', a training course for new seekers. The boys grew in the church, building godly relationships with their peers and older people, and both were involved in worship, with Mark playing the keyboard and David the drums.

I joined local government, as part of the religious advisory group within the council, and became Chair of Governors at Mark's secondary school. This meant working closely with senior management, the unions and the council. I was also a governor of one of the local primary schools.

I was busy building up the business, which was becoming very successful. This allowed us to add a couple of extensions to the house and have an excellent standard of living. We had lots of holidays – to Jamaica, Israel and Europe. I also became part of the local business group where our business was situated.

It was during this time that one of life's 'storms' came into our lives.

During the 1950s, my father had had a motorbike accident which had resulted in one of his thighs being burnt. At that time he was sent to Britain to have skin grafts on his leg. Now in 1993, the skin grafts had begun to weep. The doctors were unsure whether the cause was cancer or whether the skin grafts needed to be redone, so they decided to operate to examine the wound. He died on the operating table, but they were able to resuscitate him. I knew that the Lord would not take him like that, and was not worried when I heard. All seemed well, and he was discharged on 15th April 1993. However, I felt very uneasy in my spirit and had a feeling that something would happen. Sunday came as usual, all the families gathered at our parents' home for the celebration. Dad was outside in his vest, handkerchief-hat on and a cigarette in his hand, as he cooked the kebabs. It was the usual Michaelides Easter celebration; it seemed as if he had never been in hospital. Looking at my father, I thought I must have been imagining things; he looked so well.

But I was right. On the Tuesday after Easter Sunday, 20th April 1993, my father died unexpectedly of a heart attack, in my mother's arms, in their garden. I made all the funeral arrangements and organised the removal of my father's body from the home.

At the time my mother remarked, 'Where did you have the strength?' I only knew that, although I was full of grief, the work the Lord had done in my life enabled me to stand. What we had learned at WTC enabled us to handle this grief more healthily; I did not bury my grief, but allowed myself to grieve; I prayed through my feelings with friends who, in turn, prayed regarding the shock of my father's death, and ministered to me during this time. John was again confronted by death and, although he withdrew, it was not as severe as previously. The ministry he had had helped him to cope. We were both learning.

I was more secure in the Lord's love for me now, and could see the goodness of the Lord, even in the death of my father. The Lord did not take him on the operating table but allowed us all the pleasure of one last celebration with him. It was fitting that it was the Easter festival, about the resurrection of Jesus.

By the end of 1997 we were well established in the community, in the church and socially. However, while we were enjoying our lives, we felt something was missing. We had settled into a routine like everyone else: work, family, church and friends. Surely there was something more in our walk with the Lord? The boys were both now at university, away from home, so we had more time to think about the direction in which we wanted our lives to go.

On 1st January 1998, while we were sitting up in bed chatting about the year ahead and life in general, I suggested praying a specific prayer. It was: 'Lord, we feel we are in a rut, with You and in our lives. We want to go on with You, whatever the cost. Whatever it takes, Lord, we want You to work in our lives. Move us on and take us on.'

We were both united: we wanted more of the Lord; wanted to grow and move on in our spiritual walk, so we prayed this prayer.

Would we have prayed that prayer if we had known what the Lord would do? We are not sure, to be honest. We are just glad that we were not given that knowledge, because if we had not prayed that prayer, we would have missed out on one of the Lord's biggest blessings.

Unknown to us, praying that prayer was the beginning of a new thread of heavy black cord, being woven into the tapestry of our lives.

CHAPTER FIVE

THE GATHERING STORM

John

Having prayed that prayer with Rita, I soon forgot about what was prayed, and deep down I hoped that God would do the same. The festive season ended, with the only significant change being an increase in my waistline, and our life reverted to its usual frantic pace.

To the outside world, we seemed to be the ideal family. We were doing well and had status in the local community. I owned a business; we had a lovely detached house with a mature groomed garden in a very desirable area; outside the house stood a nice modern family car that was regularly washed and waxed. We had friends – many friends – mainly from the Baptist church we attended, and relatives from both sides of the family that got on well together. Our calendar was always full, studded with social events and activities.

However, had people known what I was going through they might have had second thoughts about the image we reflected of the 'ideal family'. At this stage of my life I was extremely busy and undertook many things, because I wanted to be part of what I felt mattered. It was a bittersweet experience; at times I would dream about what it would be like if God stopped time for a day (Joshua 10:13) so I could catch up with myself and not race around like a headless chicken.

Our business, which had been established since December 1977, had grown substantially over a period. However, we were now facing severe competition and our business profit margins were being squeezed. One major competitor decided that in selling their goods, they would absorb the cost of the value added tax (VAT) instead of passing it on to their customers. It was like committing *hara-kiri*, a suicidal act, because in those days VAT was at 17.5 per cent. Consequently, our business suffered further erosion in our profits, as we often had to match our competitor's price just to maintain our relationship with existing customers. At the same time, other competitors were openly offering cash back (brown envelopes) to buyers who ordered from them. Running a business had become very messy, and it was a daily struggle just to keep our head above water.

Also, the local government in our business area implemented major road works after receiving a substantial grant from central government. The road works would have gone on for a year, with one major arterial road closed for the duration of the project, disrupting the flow of goods to and from businesses in our area. At this stage, I felt a bit like Job in the Bible, receiving one piece of bad news after another. I became anxious and fearful, as I imagined that all my efforts to build up something might simply evaporate in front of my eyes. All my strength and energy had gone into building up the business, and I viewed it as my sole provider. God, by now, had taken second place to the company and work had become my idol and provider.

Well, not to be outdone by the council, I galvanised the Local Business Association and spearheaded a fight against this proposal.

'What do those idiots in the council know about real life?' I thought. In my fear that I would lose everything, I became furious, and I suspect I did not even think about praying to God about my problems. My venom was directed at councillors – thinking that all they did was sit on their backsides and make decisions without consulting the people and businesses they served. My sleeves were rolled up for the fight, and this took a lot of my time and energy. We raised a petition against the council's proposal, collecting thousands of signatures from businesses and residences in the area, and had the story published in the local paper.

The paper was very sympathetic to our cause and published a front-page picture of my dad and me with all the petitions in my hand. I had all my guns blazing, including a visit to the local Member of Parliament (Glenda Jackson). She was able to take up our cause and talk to members of the local government on our behalf. I believe our MP's intervention was the final straw that broke the camel's back, and the local council cancelled the project. We won the fight, but it came at a cost to my well-being, as it consumed all my mental and physical energy.

It highlighted a characteristic of mine that God had to deal with. It was a single-minded attitude that if someone, or something, came to oppose me, I would not stop until I was victorious – winning was everything. Maybe this was a subconscious trigger back to my school days, when my teacher told me that I would not achieve anything. I guess anyone who opposed me reminded me of that teacher, whose 'wise' words caused me to mentally mutilate him whenever his memory came to light. Also, I loved my status in the business community, and my role in opposing the roadwork proposal had given me a lot of personal kudos.

However, my campaign against the council was not undertaken from a God-given position of faith and strength, but from a deep-seated fear that we would lose the business. I viewed the business as my only source of provision, and this had caused me to be fearful and highly anxious. Throughout the ordeal I was extremely stressed, and nothing anyone said deterred me, keeping this matter continually in my mind. It had a detrimental effect on the quality of my sleep, and I would often get up very early to mull over the forthcoming day's events.

Outside of my work, I was also fully involved in the life of our local Baptist church. As a member of the diaconate, we went through a period where we seemed to face one issue after another. The building, which was constructed in 1906, always needed our attention. We had to juggle the church's finances so that priority was given to the most urgent needs. That was nothing compared to the people issues we had to contend with. I realised that people who wanted attention, for any reason, sucked up my energy. The diaconate meetings were getting more frequent as issues increasingly came to our attention. Often the meetings would conclude late at night. On reflection, this is one position I should have resigned from, but the allure of a leadership position kept me captive.

Finally, Rita and I were also involved with an emotional and physical healing ministry called Wholeness Through Christ (WTC). We were both members of the north-London committee, organising and helping run day seminars and teaching held in various churches. The connections we made with the brothers and sisters at WTC proved valuable when I had my mental breakdown, as they were the first to assist us in prayer and fasting, one of the significant ways used by God to turn my life around.

At home, in my daily routine, the one ritual that gave me mental rest and satisfaction was taking my dog Socs out for his daily walk. The day started just after five o'clock when I would take Socs to the local park at the end of our road. I had always wanted a large dog; after all, it would not look good for my image to have one of those little dogs that resembled a 'rat' more than a real man's dog. It would also have to obey my commands instantly and, to that end, I set out to train him. Other dog owners seemed to spend a lot of time and energy calling their dogs without success. I would see them, each hurtling towards their dog in an attempt to attach the lead around its neck. I was determined to do better; even in this area, I wanted show how successful I was compared to other dog owners. I was not going to fuss. I was determined to get Socs to sit when I said 'sit' and to walk when I said 'walk'.

However, it proved to be a greater challenge than I had envisaged, as Socs had a mind of his own and I am sure most of the time he went along just to maintain a quiet life. One command he refused to obey was, 'Socs, fetch the ball.' I would wave the yellow tennis ball in front of his eyes and say, 'Socs, this is a ball. I am going to throw it away, and you must fetch it back.'

When I did so, he would look at me with amazement, and I am sure if he could speak he would say, 'What do you think I am? A dumb dog? Fetch it yourself!'

I soon learned not to throw the ball too far because I would have to fetch it myself.

On reflection, a time that should have been fun and relaxing had become stressful, as I tried to make Socs conform to the image I wanted to portray.

Returning home from the park, Socs would settle himself in his favourite spot in our large kitchen diner and I would prepare for work. That is when I would come back down to earth, as my mind kicked into the daily tasks ahead of me.

My security and routine in what I had established and wanted to maintain were now severely shaken. God was in the process of answering our prayers in His own way, and it often felt as if I was losing my grip. From a godly perspective, one could say that they were positive changes but, if I am honest, I did not want God to answer that prayer I had half-heartedly joined-in with Rita at the beginning of the year. I was content to maintain my lifestyle and be in control of, in charge of, my life. I had been on life's treadmill ever since I got married to Rita and had continued to try and build 'the kingdom of John' according to my ways. I had one foot in the world and the other in God's kingdom.

At that time, a significant change took place that impacted our daily household routine: both our sons left for university away from home. Although Mark was older than David by sixteen months and ahead of him academically by a year, they both started their university life at the same time. Mark went to Wolverhampton University, some 180 km away, and David was even further up the motorway at Sheffield University – approximately 230 km away from London. It meant that we could not see them regularly and so the family dynamics changed overnight. I was sad, as we got on well as a family. We both missed having the boys around the house. Most nights we would try to have dinner together, exchange news, or have a hearty debate about something or other. The boys' moving away suddenly left a bit of a vacuum in our lives and it was instantly noticeable that our home was considerably quieter without them. Most people cherish the day their children move on but I was not ready for it, and suddenly everything was changing.

Another change which occurred just after the boys left home was Rita getting a full-time job at the headquarters of the Reform Synagogue of Great Britain in Finchley, north London. It was the first time in nineteen years that she had a full-time, paid job, and all credit to her. The timing was just perfect for Rita; her tasks at home became fewer, giving her a great opportunity to work in an environment that was challenging, yet comfortable and friendly. Wow, God was undoubtedly moving things around, but part of me did not like the change as I felt that my worth and value as the family's sole provider was being eroded. On reflection, I was a person who did not easily adapt to change.

I should have been grateful to God for the income that Rita was bringing in which increased our spending power. A day I remember well was 17th August 1998, when the last payment on our house mortgage was made. We had been dutifully paying-off a significant amount every month for twenty-four years, and finally the day came when we were no longer beholden to the bank. 'Hoorah!'

It was also a significant boost to our disposable income, and we could indulge in more of the things we wanted to do – what joy, what happiness! Interestingly, however, when that day finally came, rather than being grateful to God, I felt emotionally flat. Instead of celebrating, I reminisced about the fact that the mortgage had become a kind of iconic irritant that had to be destroyed. Now that I had finally managed it and gotten off that treadmill, it brought me no joy, just a feeling that I had been partly a slave to the banks who provided the finance. I felt things were shutting down on me and that my life was changing irreversibly. Unfortunately, I viewed the changes as a glass half empty, not half full. Looking back now, it makes no sense.

At the same time, I did not realise that I was experiencing a form of self-imposed sleep deprivation. Although five or six hours of sleep felt adequate, I was now waking up with a busy, irritable mind and would look at the clock animatedly for an hour before I got up to start my daily routine. I always seemed to have the energy to get up and go but, on reflection, my body was probably being stimulated with an adrenaline rush. I thought I was OK and had the stamina to face another day. I prided myself on the belief that I had the same physical constitution as the then Prime Minister of the United Kingdom, Margaret Thatcher, who would often state that she only needed four hours of sleep a night. Also, without realising or bothering to do something about it, my quiet times with God went out the window. Often to my irritation, Rita, having noticed this fact, would ask me, 'When was the last time you read your Bible?'

I would reply with a harsh voice, 'I will get round to it, leave it to me!'

In my self-made, chaotic life, God was not a priority. My walk with God had turned into a religious exercise, pretending at church that I was, in some way, spiritually attuned to God. I would go through the ritual, saying and doing the things that would show others that I was worthy of my leadership position. I was merely going through the motions of believing; I thought I knew what it meant to be a believer in Jesus Christ. But God had other ideas as His promise to me was that He would never leave nor forsake me, even if I was drifting away from Him (Deut. 31:6).

The culmination of a chaotic life and drifting away from God was that I was heading for a breakdown, and I was not aware of it. Had someone warned me (nobody did), I would most probably have laughed at them with scorn, thinking a breakdown was something that happens to other people, not me. In my arrogance, I felt I could handle pressure and stress, and that it would never get the better of me. Hindsight is an excellent thing; it challenges one's prideful thinking. Why was I so foolish, believing I was special, and immune from the dangers of life? I had heard a while earlier, the story of a senior company executive driving home from work who just stopped at a lay-by because he was feeling tired. That was it for him; he could no longer drive after his rest, and had experienced a mental breakdown. He froze there with fright, and an ambulance had to come and take him to hospital. I used to think these stories only applied to other people.

Regrettably, I can now look back and list all the signs of my oncoming mental breakdown. Unknowingly I had been suffering a form of depression over an extended period; I was always tired, continuously running on adrenaline, void of mental rest and full of anxiety. As my life became more hectic, so did my mind. I soon found myself waking up early and feeling quietly agitated about the day ahead, often with a negative attitude. Without realising it, I was becoming less tolerant of people, and snapping at them if things were not done efficiently or on time. I did not take time away to just rest, debrief and be grateful to God for the many things He had given me. Instead of being thankful, I would often grumble at God for not fixing things in my life so that I could be content. Breakfast was always rushed, and lunch was a sandwich on the go, with a lot of comfort snacks in between. The result, inevitably, was me being overweight due to an unhealthy lifestyle with little or no physical exercise.

All the while, there was something that kept me going without really wanting to change. I enjoyed the praises of men, and there were a lot of them. I enjoyed being known as a go-getter and someone who was always industrious. Church and God were the same and it was all about doing, organising, and seeing to other people's needs – a kind of pseudo-Christianity that had more to do with social connection than spiritual maturity. It meant that my spiritual walk with God was on a downward spiral. I made little time in my daily routine to read the Bible or pray. The one aspect of my life that would see my strength renewed was almost non-existent (Isa. 40:31). My prayer life consisted of a quick, 'Bless my day, bless Rita and the boys and please help the business through its difficulties.'

So my priorities had become distorted; life was more about building and maintaining the kingdom of John than the kingdom of God.

However, God had other ideas. He never stopped loving me, even when I drifted away and viewed Him as Mr Fix It, someone from whom I could demand instant solutions. I did not know He was patiently waiting to get my attention, as I was the one that needed serious fixing. I was the one running away from God, building my own idol within the community. At this point, God allowed an extreme event to take place in my life that would change me.

Rita had booked a week away in the Lake District, thinking that we both needed a well-deserved rest. Instead of being grateful for her timely initiative I was half-hearted about the trip and already grumbling. Didn't she know that there was so much to do, and so many things needed my attention? I must have been sending Rita signals that this holiday was ill-timed. I was entirely selfish not thinking about her needs, and was taking the fun out of something that she was looking forward to.

An accident occurred at home that resulted in an emergency run to the hospital. About a month before our holiday, while cooking rice at dinner time, Rita accidentally poured the hot water from the pan onto her left hand. She was in absolute agony, and we rushed to the emergency department of the local hospital. She was quickly seen to as it was evident that her injuries were serious. At one stage they tried to remove the wedding ring from her burnt finger, but could not. The nurse suggested that the only way to remove it would be to cut into the ring. This distressed Rita even more and she cried out, 'I don't want to lose my ring!' Eventually they managed to remove the ring and treat her burnt hand. She was given a strong painkiller to help her sleep through the night.

Watching all this unfold, I felt the tremendous pain she went through, but also a sense of helplessness as the whole event was outside my control. The accident evoked memories of my mother, who died of cancer in 1984 after having suffered for about six months. Unconsciously my mind related Rita's accident and hospital trip to my mother's death – an event in my life that was unresolved. I had not adequately grieved my mother's untimely death, and had not been to a hospital since, but now the whole event surfaced again, and this time I could not suppress it anymore. Rita's accident and memories of my mother's painful death were the final straws that broke the camel's back.

CHAPTER SIX

THE STORM BREAKS

Rita

Once we said our prayer on 1st January 1998, I forgot completely about it. Life proceeded as normal. The boys were at university, and I was enjoying my administration work with the Reform Synagogue of Great Britain. It was good to feel like I was beginning a career. Working full-time was a little bit of a shock to the system but, with the boys away and John out all day, there hadn't been any good reason to be at home. The extra money came in useful now that both boys were in university and I thought maybe we could go away more, or go out. John had won his fight with the council and, from my perspective, life was looking good. We had entered into a different season and adjusted quite well – or so I thought.

But John had other ideas. He was now over the business, and had begun looking for other jobs in all parts of the country. I was fine with that, even though I had just started a new job – I was always up for a challenge – but he was not getting very far, and it was hard to see his disappointment. Meanwhile, he was becoming more and more unsettled and emotionally dependent on me. It should have been a good time for us, two incomes and the boys settled and happy. It was meant to be 'our time', but it was gradually becoming more and more stressful, especially for me. I was busy trying to learn a new job and adapt to a new way of life but, at the back of my mind, I always thought of John. He was unhappy, struggling, and often not thinking straight.

Sometimes I was resentful and angry at him. Couldn't he just be content? Couldn't he just enjoy this season? I resented the pressure I felt under and his negativity and dullness. But then I would feel guilty; after all, I was not the one who had had to work so hard all these years, carrying the pressures of running a business. Thus I concluded that he just needed to get away. The fight with the council and the business had taken a lot out of him, physically and mentally. He needed to have a change of scenery – or so I thought. It was time for us to take a deep breath, to re-connect, have some good food, wine and fun. Little did I know that the change of scenery would be the catalyst for him to come apart. Would I have booked it if I knew? Not sure, to be honest. Anyway, on the recommendation of a friend, I booked a very luxurious guest house in the Lake District for August. Once I had booked the place, I felt better but, as you know from John's account, he was not too happy. I dismissed his reaction, thinking once we were there he would be fine.

Sometime in July of that year the Lord gave me a picture of a small boat sailing through a narrow canyon with tall mountains on each side. I shared the picture with John, and I remember saying that we were the sailing boat and that, if we were not careful, we would crash into the mountains. He shrugged his shoulders and I thought no more about it. I believe now that the Lord was warning us. Maybe if we had taken time to pray and think about what the Lord was saying, we might not only have averted what was to come, but dealt with the issues differently. Maybe the Lord was giving John, or both of us, an opportunity to deal with the issues in our lives that were ungodly, or hindering us, before He stepped in and did it. Many times we see in the Old Testament that the Lord gives His people warnings to repent before judgement comes; I wonder if we were being given a similar warning. But I just filed it in my mind, and got on with life.

From my perspective, the visit to the hospital before our holiday was a disaster, not just because of my hand but because of the effect it had on John. At the hospital I could see John, as it were, almost disappear before my eyes. I know that sounds like an exaggeration, but I could see in his eyes that he had withdrawn deep within himself. My accident, my pain, and the rush to the hospital were all too much for him. He retreated, and a 'front' was put up. Even while I was struggling with the pain, I registered all this and pushed it to the back of my mind. All he needed was an enjoyable and restful holiday.

My hand healed well and I began to prepare for our holiday. We went shopping one Saturday to buy some much-needed clothes for John; it was like going shopping with a child. His mind was all over the place, he could not make any decisions, and he had a dull look in his eyes. I wonder what the shop assistant thought of our conversation, which went something like this.

'John, do you like this shirt?' I'd ask as I picked a shirt from the rack.

'Sure,' he replied, in a dull monotone voice, as he looked out the window.

'But, John, you are not even looking at it,' I replied impatiently.

'I can see it in the reflection in the window,' he said, still looking outside, which was a blatant lie, as the window was nowhere near enough to get a reflection of anything.

'No you can't. Will you just turn round and look at it,' I angrily hissed at John. I was trying to keep my voice low as there were other people around us.

He slowly turned around with a glazed look in his eyes. 'Looks great,' he said, with as much enthusiasm as a child visiting the dentist.

I just shoved it in his hands and said, 'Just go and try it on,' and he did what he was told, as if I were his mother and he a child.

This was just one example of how John was, yet I still thought all he needed was a good rest. In the back of my mind I remembered the other occasions when he had acted like this, but I ignored them, not believing this was the same thing. Maybe I just could not face the possibility that it was happening again. So I acted as if everything was alright. I put on a front for the boys, who were home from university at the time. Inside, I was battling with fear, was very unsettled, and felt pressured.

Smiling brightly at the boys, as if all was well, we set off on a sunny Monday morning in August. John was quiet and just went through the motions. Usually when we go on long journeys, we put on teaching CDs, but this time I played worship songs. Throughout the journey I chatted on brightly, trying to impart some anticipation to John, to give him something to get excited about. But it was a very ordinary journey.

We arrived, and the place was lovely. The view from our room was stunning. The green, lush mountains, the summer flowers around the guest house and, for once, blue skies. Despite John, I was very excited. Here, I thought, things would work out; with God's creation all around us, good food and wine, my John would come back – I was living in a fool's paradise.

The next day, the nightmare began for me. John was like a walking zombie – that is the only way I can describe it. It was as if something had sucked out his very being and left only his body behind. Often people joke to get someone's attention by tapping on the other person's head saying, 'Hey! Anyone in there?' It was exactly like that with John but, in this case, there was no one there. Even now, as I write this, I am struggling to express how he was.

We went for a walk in front of the beautiful lake, and I tried to jolly him along. 'Look,' I would say, 'how stunning is this?' He would just nod.

When I would make suggestions as to what to do, he would just shrug his shoulders without saying anything.

Finally I snapped, shouting, 'What is the matter with you?' while I was trying to suppress the fear and panic that were welling up from deep inside me. To my horror, John started to cry; I had never seen John cry before.

'I don't know,' he said, 'I don't know.' I could not get any sense from him.

It was a bizarre situation. All around us was tranquillity, the lake so still, reflecting the brightness of the sun, the smell of the summer flowers, with only the buzzing of the bees as sound. The gentle sounds of laughter and chatter as people walked past us. Between us, as if we were in our own special bubble, there was no such tranquillity, only fear, panic and anxiety.

I swallowed my fear and went into action mode, 'Let's pray about it.' There beside the lake, I prayed. I prayed for peace to come in, and over, him; prayed for his heart and mind to be still. To be honest, I do not know exactly what I prayed – I just prayed. I wanted so much for him to be well that when he said he felt better, I believed him and thought it was all over.

But as the next few days unfolded, he wasn't better; he was getting worse. So we prayed again. I would go into 'prayer ministry mode' and asked him what the Lord was showing him or what came to mind. Often he would share some incidents from his childhood, or remember some unforgiveness he had against someone, or a traumatic event. At Wholeness Through Christ, we had been taught the Four Quadrants as a guide for how to pray into situations. The Four Quadrants are: bondages to be broken, sins to be forgiven, the deliverance of spirits and healing. So applying what I had learned and experienced I prayed into each of those situations. At the end of each prayer time, I would think, 'That's it, now he is OK,' as John would have some respite and peace. But the next day he went back to being the same, so we would pray again. He was eating very little, and had periods of just switching off, where I could not reach him.

Even though we kept talking and praying it did not seem to make any difference. Meanwhile, I was trying hard to pretend that all was well in front of others. We were having breakfast and dinner at the guest house so, to compensate for his state, I would overreact and be super friendly. This was very unlike me and put me under even more strain. I was battling with my emotions; on the one hand, I was angry at John that our holiday was being ruined. Why couldn't he just snap out of it? It was not fair. On the other hand, I was desperately afraid. Previous occasions, when he behaved similarly, were never as bad as this. In those times, I could at least reach him, but this was on a new, different level. I felt alone, not knowing where to turn.

Our stay in the guest house finished on Friday, and we had planned to drive to Bakewell. John seemed a little better and so we set off, with him at the wheel. It was a long drive and very traumatic. The country roads were windy and often on a cliff edge. Furthermore, John spent most of the time crying, saying he just wanted to die, to plunge the car over the edge. Again, fighting my panic, I managed to get John to stop; we found a parking spot and pulled over.

I immediately started praying, and I remember seeing in the Spirit, a can of worms over John. To me, that spoke of demonic involvement so, at the roadside, I prayed for deliverance from every unclean spirit I could think of, and maybe I did more harm than good, but it was all I could do. I was like a shooter shooting at anything that moved. John could not explain why he was feeling so bad, why he was crying and sobbing in utter despair. I was dealing with my own demons of fear and panic – 'What was I going to do with him?' – but at the same time I had a deep faith and conviction that the Lord would sort it out – John only needed more prayer; there was nothing the Lord could not do; and surely it was better to have these things out, rather than suppressed.

Cars were passing us by, and the day was getting on. We had not booked a hotel in Bakewell and, if we did not hurry, we might not get a place. Slowly, John calmed down and seemed a little better. He insisted he was OK to drive and we set off. I knew, without a shadow of a doubt, that we were in the centre of a spiritual battle. Knowing that praise is a powerful spiritual weapon I put on the worship CD and blasted the car with the songs.

We finally reached Bakewell where we parked the car. Strangely, John was calmer and, while not himself, was able to act in a more normal way. He was still not able to make any decisions, so I booked a country hotel, all done in Laura Ashley wallpaper and print.

We checked in and went to our room. John did not want to eat and, even though it was only around 6.30 p.m., he wanted to go to bed. No sooner was he in bed than he fell asleep. It was such a deep sleep that it seemed as if he was not breathing, and I had to lean very close to his mouth to feel his breath.

I quickly rang our friends, John and Helen, in London. Trying not to cry or panic, I told them what was happening and asked them to pray. We agreed that I would bring John around to them tomorrow afternoon, after we got back to London. It was still early and I did not want to disturb John, so I took my Bible and went down to the lounge to read. I could neither eat nor read; my stomach was in knots, and my mind all over the place.

I went back upstairs an hour or so later; John was still asleep in the same position that I had left him. It felt eerie looking at him. It seemed to me that his sleep was unnatural and, suddenly, I collapsed. I remember rushing into the bathroom, shutting the door and falling like a heap on the floor. I crawled to the furthest corner of the room, and howled and cried as I had never done before. So that my cries would not be heard, I stuffed towels in my mouth. My world was falling apart in front of my eyes. What was going to happen to John? What about the boys? What about me? At that moment, I felt that I had lost John, and he was my world. I could not understand what was happening. Why were the prayers not working? Where was the power for change? Why was he not only not healed, but worse? Doubt now joined fear and panic; my faith in God's healing power was shaking. The fear and panic I had suppressed came out of me and filled the room – the bright, shining bathroom seemed full of darkness – I shrank even further into the corner to hide from it all. I do not know how long I stayed there, but eventually I got up and went to bed. I was so exhausted that I managed to sleep. John just kept sleeping, unaware of what was happening.

In the morning John insisted he was fine to drive back to London and, still without food, we set off. It was only by God's grace and protection that we got back to London in one piece; John was crying all the way home. I would offer to drive, but he would not let me and, fearful of making him worse, I let him. Once again, I played praise songs and prayed constantly while John was fighting thoughts of suicide.

As we were approaching home, I remember giving John a stern warning: 'You had better act normal. I don't want the boys seeing you like this.' Somehow he managed to pull himself together. We pulled into the drive and I put on my 'everything is fine' look.

We told the boys what a great time we'd had, how beautiful it was, and that we would love to go again. All lies, but there was no way I would allow the boys to know what had actually happened; that their father was falling apart. And anyway, he would be better after we had seen John and Helen, wouldn't he? What was the point of worrying them? It was only much later that it was necessary to tell them what was happening.

Meanwhile, we unloaded the car, took the cases upstairs and I started to unpack. John went straight to the bedroom and lay down on the bed. I went downstairs and, again, put on a front and told the boys that Dad was tired and resting, and that later in the afternoon we were going to see John and Helen. All these things we usually did anyway so, for the boys, everything was normal.

In the afternoon, we went to see John and Helen and began to pray. As we prayed John began to manifest, demons were throwing him around on the floor. John and Helen commanded the spirits to come out. At one stage they asked John, speaking directly to the demonic spirit, 'What is your name?' and John replied, 'Legion.'

We had all had experience in deliverance, both in commanding and being delivered, but we could see that this was altogether a different ballgame. John (not my John) said that he thought that my John was having a nervous breakdown and I shouted at him, 'No, it's just spiritual, just healing he needs.' I could not accept it was anything but spiritual, as I did not have faith in any other type of healing. If it was spiritual, then we could pray him through it and he would be fine. After all, that was my experience. Every time I had problems with my mind, prayer was given, and I was fine, so surely it must be the same for everyone? Later, when John exhibited all the classic signs of a major breakdown, including depression, suicidal thoughts and insomnia, I realised how right he was.

Helen was weeping at seeing my John in such a state. In fact, we were all a little shocked and traumatised by it. Whatever was prayed must have made a difference because John was calmer, and no longer being thrown about. We stayed for a while, and then left.

When we got home, John again went straight to the bedroom. Again I told the boys that Dad was just tired from the drive. I was tired, and struggled to keep my fears and emotions in check. In the evening, I drove the boys to a party, pretending all the time that it was just another normal day in the Helvadjian household.

John did not eat that night. During the evening, he came down and grabbed a yogurt. He said that a voice told him that he had to eat something. My nerves were frayed, but I suppressed my feelings and went on as normal, putting the washing in the machine, shopping for food, and planning the week ahead.

The next day, John seemed much better – almost normal – so we decided to go to John and Helen's church, as John was preaching. On the drive there, I cannot remember whether it was John or me, but we had a picture of a fat, sleek, coiled-up black snake. Immediately, we knew that it represented us. We had grown fat and sleek on the praises of men. Many people in our church looked up to us. We were the golden couple, seen as spiritually higher than them and we lapped it all up. But, in reality, we were shallow, proud and arrogant, and no better than anyone else. When we realised this, we knew that we had to leave the church. I know to some people that seemed strange. Why leave? Why the sudden decision? But we both came to the same conclusion: we knew, however odd it sounded, that it was the right thing to do.

We felt so convicted about leaving that we rang the pastor that day and made an appointment to see him that afternoon. We explained that we thought it was time for us to move, that it was nothing that he, or the church, had done but the season for us had changed. He was very gracious, although I knew he did not fully understand why we were doing this. To be honest, we did not fully understand what was going on either. We left with his blessing, and never went back. In hindsight, maybe we should have gone back, at least for a service or a deacons' meeting, to explain and say our goodbyes in person. I know we hurt some people because of our sudden departure, for which we are sorry.

The boys were already going to another church, and they knew that we were not happy at our church. So when we told them we had left, it did not come as too much of a surprise to them. Once again everything seemed quite normal.

The coming week was the boys' last week before going back to university. During the week, John was almost his normal self. He still spoke and ate less, but not enough to notice anything different about him. I knew, though, that he was still not a hundred per cent right; I thought time would sort that out.

It had been a strain acting as if all was well during that week. So when the boys went back to university, I began to relax a little and allow myself to think that the problems with John were over; we were getting back to normal; our prayers had worked and, although we might never know what had caused this episode, it was over.

Before leaving our church, I had promised to speak at one of the ladies' events and, not wanting to let them down, I still went. After coming home from church that evening, John told me that he still did not have any peace in his mind. He was struggling to hold it together. After feeling that things were behind us, I felt sick in my stomach that John's negative thoughts had surfaced again, and was angry with him. Surely, after all the prayer and ministry, he must be fine. Was he not walking in the newness of what the Lord had done? John said he would fight it, that he would get better. These were words I needed to hear. However, I did not realise just how much of a fight it would be or how much worse he would get before he got better.

CHAPTER SEVEN

THE HEALING BEGINS

RITA

Have you ever tried to squash a whole lot of stuff into a tin? You press and press all the stuff down, carefully placing the lid on top, tucking in any loose bits, only to have the lid ping open a couple of moments later, and all the stuff you painstakingly pressed down explodes all over the place. You pick up the pieces, scattered all over the place, often missing the bits that rolled under the table, and start all over again, this time, leaving some bits out, so the lid stays in place.

It was as if the lid of John's mind had just flipped open, and all the issues he had suppressed and pressed down during his life, exploded. We spent the next few months gathering the bits together; but instead of just putting them back as they were, we confronted the issues, bringing them before the Lord as we dealt with them. Slowly, the pieces were put back, healed and restored.

After the boys went back to university, John went downhill very quickly. I believe the Lord's grace enabled John to hold it together while they were around. I was so glad they never saw their dad descend from the confident, strong man and father whom they depended on, who looked after and protected them, to the shivering, shaking man who could not say 'boo' to a goose. They never saw him walking around the house in a trance as he muttered to himself, or curling himself in a corner, or saw the vacant look in his eyes, or witnessed the raw pain he was going through. It was not until the end of November that we visited the boys at their universities to tell them that their dad had had a nervous breakdown. By then, John, while not wholly healed, was at least slowly on his way back up, and we felt we wanted to tell the boys at a time when we could reassure them that John was on the mend, and they could see for themselves that their dad had a sense of normality.

We had been involved with prayer ministry for some years now, and so we understood that issues are always better dealt with than suppressed. Even through the darkest times in his illness, John did not want to avoid dealing with issues, or suppress them anymore. He wanted to face them, however painful, and deal with them once and for all. In so doing, John decided not to go down the medical route by consulting a doctor. I agreed with him, knowing that he would be diagnosed, then medicated which, we felt, would only deal with the symptoms and not the root causes of his mental illness. Also, it was possible that once John was stabilised on medication it would be tough for him to come off it, and could have resulted in a lifetime of dependency on medication. However, there was, and is, a considerable cost in choosing this route; the decision was not an easy one to make, but we were united.

One of John's closest friends, who was not a Christian but had known him since primary school, remarked that John was a courageous man to go through the breakdown without medical help, and he felt it was the wrong decision. Please note here that we are in no way advocating that people should not seek medical help, or that prayer ministry is the only way. When Jesus healed people in the Bible, He did so in a variety of ways. No two healings were the same. We are all individuals and the Lord deals with us individually. It was a decision we made for ourselves, believing that we were being led by the Lord. There were times, though, when John felt the pain in his head was so severe that he could not take it anymore. He tried to contact a general practitioner (GP), or a Christian counsellor, but each time he tried, something happened to prevent him getting through, as if God had placed a roadblock in the way. Either his GP was on holiday, or the phone line to the counsellor was always engaged. Eventually, after much prayer, we felt convinced that it was not the enemy putting blocks in John's way, but the Lord. He wanted John to seek Him more deeply, so that his healing would come through prayer and the word of the Lord. He wanted to build-up John's faith.

The decision to seek only God in John's healing came at a considerable cost. For John, it meant that he experienced severe mental pain for long periods, without any relief. For quite a long time he hardly slept at night, existing on only a few hours of sleep, or none at all. He told me once that the voices in his head were like a never-ending broken record, giving him no rest. Knowing this, and watching him, was very painful for me. I was often at a loss, not knowing how I could help him. The voices were telling him to run away from home and live on the streets, that by running away, he would be free. Other voices would tell him to kill himself, so that the pain in his head would go away. He saw everything in life negatively, as if through a magnifying glass; minor issues were greatly catastrophised. I only had to say that I had a headache and he would fear a brain tumour. The cost for me was seeing my wonderful, confident husband – who loved me and looked after his family – reduced to a shell of a man, wasting away before my eyes, in terrible mental pain.

By the end of August, John was not functioning well. He was extremely fearful, mentally unstable, and could not make any decisions.

His favourite pastimes, like good food and fine wine, all went out the window. He lost his appetite and was just eating enough to stay alive, so he lost a lot of weight. At work, he usually commanded the operations, doing a hundred tasks at once, but now he was a total wreck. When issues arose, he would cover his ears with his hands, and cower in a corner, unable to confront them.

It was only in the last couple of years that his sister, Hilda, who worked with John, told me that he used to go into her office, wrap his arms around himself, and rock backwards and forwards. At times like this, she, like us, doubted that John would ever be healed. However, Hilda was amazing; she was my partner in his healing, and she was on the same page with us. She encouraged him to use scripture to fight, and to stand, with faith. I often called her John's Day Nurse, and I was his Night Nurse. It was a blessing that they owned the business, and that both John's father and sister, who worked with him, were believers. They prayed for him, and stepped in and covered for him.

From the beginning, we knew we were in a battle, and were united in fighting this together. There were very real demonic influences that were seeking to rob and destroy us. I found myself going into battle mode. A gritty determination arose in me that we would not be deprived, we were going to fight for our family, nothing was going to destroy us, and I was going to make sure that John fought too.

As I look back, I was like a lioness protecting her cub, fighting against anyone who would come near. I even fought against John, not allowing him to 'rest', pushing him to fight the voices in his head, to face his fears. I would not allow him to have self-pity parties, or to crawl away and hide. I nagged him to eat, take vitamins – especially the B supplements –

to read his Bible, learn scripture and sometimes, to just 'get over it'.

I knew that our God would triumph, but there were times when I was fighting from sheer desperation and tremendous fear, not faith. During such times, I realised how my upbringing had prepared me for this moment. Self-reliance, independence, strength, resourcefulness and the ability to rise to confront any challenge, nurtured in me as I grew up, were crucial. Although I was crumbling inside, miraculously, I managed to hold it together.

One of the most important and fundamental things that happened early on in the journey was a verse the Lord gave me. I was hanging out the washing, and the Lord brought Psalm 118:18 to mind: *'The LORD has chastened me severely, but He has not given me over to death.'* I knew that this was from the Lord, to comfort and encourage me; that the Lord was in control and, though He was disciplining us, it would not lead to death, either spiritual or physical. It became a word that I held close to my heart, especially as John was often suicidal. This verse was like a corset holding me together. When I felt overwhelmed and the fears crowded in, I would proclaim this verse, wielding it like a sword, putting into practice Ephesians 6:17.

John was fearful, even of his own shadow. The voices in his head told him that it was dangerous to go outside and he was afraid of being alone. Left to himself, he would just stay in bed, huddled under the covers. He could not handle the outside world. One issue was that I was working, and I was not going to stop. Rightly or wrongly, I knew that if I let him do just want he wanted, he would not get better. If I allowed him to slip into self-pity, I believed I would lose him forever. I gave him tough love, with no sympathy, and did not make any allowances for him. Looking back, I probably was too tough, but I felt he had to face his fears not give in to them; he had to fight for his freedom. By going out to work, I forced John to face his fears, to go outside, and go to work where he would not be alone. Often, after not sleeping all night, he would still get up at 6.30 a.m. to go to work. How John ever got there safely was a mystery. Without sleep, feeling suicidal, and in fast London traffic, it was a miracle each day he drove to work. Some days, he would leave in the morning, and I would wonder whether I would see him again. While I struggled, I held on tightly to Psalm 118:18 that the Lord had given me. Some may think it was foolhardy to let him do this in his condition, but I knew that I had to trust the Lord. Part of John's healing required him to fight as well; I could not keep him locked up safely indefinitely.

Because we had left the church so suddenly, most people were unaware of what was happening, or that John was ill. Even so, the phone was silent. Hardly anyone kept in contact with us after we left; just a few people. We realised that the relationships we had were, in fact, mainly business relationships, with no foundation. Our lives had changed from a hectic social and church life – our house buzzing with people – to silence and loneliness. Suddenly the house seemed oppressive where once it had been full of light, laughter and vibrancy, and I felt the loss acutely. Even though John was better some days than others, I could not risk inviting anyone over. He was very unpredictable and could go from being 'normal' to morose and silent in moments. We only saw a few close friends who knew and understood the journey we were on. The family realised something was going on and that John was not himself, but not the full extent of the situation. To be able to cope, I shut the world out; that way I did not have to pretend that everything was OK. I smiled at the neighbours, made excuses to friends and kept up the pretence that we were fine. We did not go to church but we did not give up meeting with believers, as the writer of Hebrews 10:25 states, regularly meeting with a few of our close friends.

I had been in my new job for about five months when John became ill. It was a good environment to work in, and the people were great. Because John was so fearful and dependent on me, he would ring me at least five or six times a day, sometimes to check I was OK, or to tell me how he was feeling and what was happening. It was hard trying to keep focused on work with the constant calls, and I thought I was not performing to the best of my ability with all the pressure I was under. I was in a small, open-plan office yet, amazingly, no one seemed to notice or remark about the calls. Being at work enabled me to have some sense of normality. I was working in the Youth Division and having young people around me helped. No one at work knew what was happening, which again helped; they treated me as if all was well. If I had had to be with John 24/7, I am not sure how I would have coped. I was amazed – and this was pure grace – that at the end of the year, when I had my performance review with my manager, he could not speak highly enough about my work.

One book that was vital in our journey was *Living Free* by Dr Neil T. Anderson; we still have it after all these years. I am not sure how it came to our attention, but I bought it and urged John to read it. It unlocked so much for him, and he read it a few times – a miracle in itself; for John to read a book was unheard of. We understood all about dealing with root issues but this book seemed to reach John, and he was able to understand more about his issues. One chapter speaks of how to deal with fear: how to analyse it, how to face it, and how to overcome it. At the end of the book, it speaks of 'Steps to Freedom in Christ'. Armed with our Wholeness Through Christ knowledge, our experiences and this book, we started to pick up the pieces that had spilled out when the 'lid' of John's mind flipped open. As the Holy Spirit brought past situations to mind for John, we prayed into them. We exposed the lies of the enemy, we came against any legal right the enemy had to harass John, and then we prayed healing into the issue. That was how we dealt with the situations that surfaced.

One unresolved, suppressed issue was John's mother's death. It was now 1998, and she had been dead for over fourteen years, having died at the young age of fifty-three. John had never allowed himself to grieve, but grief was not the only emotion that he had suppressed; there was also anger, at God for taking her, and at the medical profession. He harboured resentment, bitterness and unforgiveness towards the doctors who had dealt with his mother. One could say that John was right to feel all these things; the doctors had given her a clean bill of health when, in fact, cancer had spread from her breast to her bones. By the time the bone cancer was discovered, it was too far advanced for any effective treatment and, six months later, she died.

But John's sinful reactions gave the devil the legal right to come and cause havoc, especially his unforgiveness. In the parable of the Unmerciful Servant that Jesus spoke of in Matthew 18, we are told that the servant was handed over to the tormentors until payment was made. When we do not forgive, we also are handed over to the tormentors.

From our experience, I would go so far as to say that most, if not all, spiritual and mental torment is the result of unforgiveness. In the Lord's Prayer, we ask the Lord to forgive us 'as we forgive others'. And in Matthew 6:14–15 Jesus made it very clear that if we do not forgive others, we will not be forgiven. The only thing that releases us from the tormentors is forgiveness. It was now time for John to deal with this.

When he came home one day, I told him it was time to confront those emotions, and he painfully agreed. I remember him sitting on the floor, in the corner against the radiator, as he poured out his grief and anger against the Lord for taking his mother. He wept and shouted to God, and I could hear his anger and frustration coming out as he let his heavenly Father know precisely where he was at. It was raw and painful for John to go through, and hard for me to hear him in such pain, but we knew that it was so necessary for his healing. Suppressed grief can do so much untold damage to our minds and bodies and, if not healthily dealt with, can lead to a spirit of heaviness, as mentioned in Isaiah 61:3. It can build up inside of us, until it erupts like a volcano, with destructive results.

Once John had expressed all he could, I asked the Holy Spirit to bring healing into all the hurts he had experienced from losing his mother. The hardest part for John was yet to come – letting go of all those negative and sinful attitudes and forgiving people, especially the doctors. We did not rush it but, when he was ready, I took him through a prayer asking the Lord's forgiveness for holding resentment, bitterness and grudges against all doctors involved, and against God. First, he repented of his anger against them and God; I kept praying for the peace of the Lord and his healing as John went through this. Then, when he was ready, I took him through a prayer forgiving the doctors who were involved. He found it hard, but he finally forgave them and released them from his unforgiveness. Lastly, I came against all spirits of fear and death, which would have come in, and commanded them to go in Jesus' name. By this time, John was very tired and drained, as often happens with prayer ministry; it can be like having a heart operation. John will always have the memory of how his mother died and the events leading up to it, but he can now remember without all the pain and negative emotions. It is like having a scar on one's finger; we can look at it and remember what caused it, we can touch it, but there is no pain as it has healed.

Another 'piece' that the Lord showed us was the negative words spoken over, and to, John. Proverbs 18:21 tells us that the tongue has the power of life and death. Words are vehicles which can carry either blessings or curses. Proverbs 12:18a says, *There is one who speaks like the piercings of a sword,'* and Psalm 64:3 says, *'Who sharpen their tongue like a sword, and bend their bows to shoot their arrows – bitter words.'*

Remember the old saying: 'Sticks and stones will break my bones, but names will never hurt me.' Well, that is not true; sometimes words are more hurtful and stay with us for a long time, if not forever, if they are not dealt with. Especially words spoken by those in authority, like a teacher or parent, for example.

The particular negative words spoken over John were when his teacher told him that he would 'never amount to much in life'. These words caused a deep wound in John, which resulted in him being driven by the need to prove that teacher wrong, and to crave success. The words also put him under pressure to perform and succeed in all areas of his life, which was a heavy burden. Additionally, negative words created shame in John because this statement was made about him publicly, in the classroom. Both the drive to perform and the shame had been with him since that time.

We exposed the lie that 'he would not mount up to much' and declared the truth that he was God's workmanship created in Christ Jesus to do good works, which God prepared in advance for him to do (Eph. 2:10). John repented of believing and agreeing with the lie. Then, in Jesus' name, we broke the power of those words over John and declared them to have no more effect on him. John repented of making the inner vow that he would prove the teacher wrong. We asked the Lord to come and heal all the areas that had been wounded.

Each 'piece' that the Lord showed us had spilled out was put back – cleaned, restored and healed. Meanwhile, I was physically and mentally getting very tired. I was not sleeping too well either and, most nights, I had to go and sleep in one of the other bedrooms because John was so restless. I was cooking a meal each night and trying to encourage John to eat but, at the same time, I was finding it difficult myself to eat. Each morning I would wake up feeling nauseated, with a huge knot in my stomach. Whenever any doubts came in, I would fiercely throw them out, not because I was super-spiritual but because I was too fearful to think of John not being healed.

One evening one of our friends rang me. 'Hi, Rita,' he began. 'How is John?'

'About the same,' I replied. We had known this friend for many years and I was grateful for his concern.

'You know, Rita,' he continued, 'I am worried about John. You know if he does not seek treatment he can go mad. I have seen it happen to other people.'

Now, I know he was speaking from genuine concern – we all knew how bad John was – but I *really, really* did not need to hear that.

I thanked him for his concern and put the receiver down, shaking with fear and overwhelmed by doubt.

I immediately rang Helen, pouring out to her what this friend had said, and asking her, 'Are we right to keep going as we are, or should I get him help? I don't know what to do.'

'No, you are doing fine, Rita,' Helen reassured me, reminding me of the Lord's promises to us, reminding me of the Lord's faithfulness and, as she spoke, faith was slowly being poured back into me, pushing all fear and doubts away.

Then I remembered what Helen had said to me when I questioned why the Lord had told us to leave the church when all this started. It was to leave us alone. She shared that, in the healing of Jairus' daughter in Luke 8, Jesus only took Peter, John and James with Him into the room, leaving all the doubters outside. I realised that on our journey, we needed to surround ourselves with people of faith. We needed to keep people out who doubted the Lord and His power to heal. I am not saying that none of the people in our church would have believed, but there were many there who did not believe in God's healing power for today. Also, I could not handle hearing too many different voices as we journeyed on this very narrow path.

John was also working and fighting hard for his healing. He found scriptures that were helpful and learnt them.

I would often hear him around the house, proclaiming them in a very loud voice, and I knew that he was fighting the voices and thoughts in his head. We were both learning how to use the word of God, the sword of the Spirit.

I was not too proud to seek help; I contacted everyone that I thought could help, even if we had not been in touch for years. John and I have never believed that God just heals us where we are; He sometimes does but, often, one has to travel to receive healing. After all, the people in Jesus' time travelled all over the place to find Him. One couple we knew, who were the heads of Wholeness Through Christ for the north London region, had moved to Birmingham. We valued their wisdom and experience, so we made our way to Birmingham.

CHAPTER EIGHT

BREAKTHROUGH

Rita

You often hear that during times of difficulty, sorrow or grief, people will find time for laughter. Some triggered memory or incident happens that releases the pressure of the situation and there is laughter. You may wonder how people can laugh when they are going through difficult times, but I can understand. There were times during John's illness when we laughed at ourselves, or at the situation we found ourselves in. The journey to Birmingham was such an occasion and, even as I write this, I am smiling.

One result of John's illness was that he was often totally compliant with what I said, like a mother giving instructions to a child, and he agreed to us going to see Jack and Jean in Birmingham. He had begun to see some improvements from what we had prayed to date, and he was eager for more. After obtaining a couple of days' leave, we set off to Birmingham; John was driving and we had our usual praise CDs on. I am not sure at what part of the journey it happened, but we got a flat tyre. It was very unusual; in all our travels, through all our years of marriage, I don't remember having a flat tyre.

John pulled over and began to change the tyre; he was not happy. Even though he had agreed to go to Birmingham, he was now grumbling about the whole idea. I just sat in the car, and helped whenever I could, but I began to smile inwardly. I had a sense that this was a tactic from the enemy, to try and put us off, to make us lose our peace, and to bring disunity between us. Some may think that viewing a flat tyre as a spiritual attack is stretching things too far. However, we are told in 1 Peter 5:8 that our enemy the devil prowls around like a roaring lion looking for someone to devour. The devil is always looking for opportunities to harass and annoy us, to try and steer us off course. I started to pray; if the enemy was trying to stop us from going to Birmingham, it meant that we were heading for a significant breakthrough, something he did not want us to have.

John managed to change the tyre and we resumed our journey, but he was getting angry about the whole trip, and his anger was directed at me. He became agitated and insulted me, saying, 'You have terrible legs. You are not even pretty, you're ugly. What did I ever see in you?' and so on.

His face and tone of voice were rude and slightly abusive, but all I could do was laugh, but inwardly, not wanting to antagonise him further. I found it all so funny. I knew that it was the demons in him talking, trying to hurt me, targeting my insecurities, trying to make me angry at John, and to cause division between us. This was even more confirmation that we were on the right track. These particular demons knew that their time was up, and they were fighting their corner. They did not succeed; I just kept my face neutral and my laughter within me and, because I did not react, John eventually stopped. Most people would not find it funny to have insults thrown at them but I found the whole situation amusing, and smiled throughout the rest of the journey.

We spent the afternoon with Jack and Jean, sharing with them all that had transpired to date. They listened intently, and decided that they would pray for John after dinner that night. I spent the rest of the afternoon with Jean, helping her to prepare the meal while John spoke to Jack.

After dinner, we gathered together and waited on the Lord. They asked John questions about his family and past generations, and it became clear there was a lot of fear in his bloodline. This was understandable, considering the Armenian genocide. John's parents, particularly his mother, were very fearful. John had not been allowed to have a bicycle, for example, in case he fell over or had an accident. Everything was planned around keeping the family safe. As children of the Lord, we are told to trust and not fear. We are told in 1 John 4:18 that fear brings torment, another key to why John was in such a tormented mental state. He had not only inherited the tendency for fear from his forefathers, but also he had compounded it through his own choices.

Fear is the opposite of faith and produces bad fruit in our lives. Often fear comes with self-reliance, independence, and the tendency to trust in man. Jeremiah 17:5 states that cursed is the one who trusts in man, who depends on flesh for his strength. With independence comes pride, and often arrogance. In the Bible, we are told that God opposes the proud (Jas 4:6), and that pride comes before a fall (Prov. 18:12). These were three areas for Jack and Jean to pray into: fear, pride, and independence, in both John and his forefathers.

They began to pray, asking John to stand in the gap for his forefathers: to confess their sins of fear, pride, and independence. Standing in the place of our forefathers and confessing is a biblical principle that we can apply. There are many occasions in the Bible when this was done: for example, the prayer of Daniel in Daniel chapter 9 or Nehemiah's prayer in Nehemiah chapter 1. By confessing the sins of our forefathers, we are effectively removing the legal ground for the devil to come and attack us. As believers, we do not suffer the punishment of our forefather's sins – the Bible tells us that each person is responsible for their actions – but we can suffer the consequences of their sins. The sins of John's forefathers allowed a curse to operate in his bloodline and, when John began to act in the same way, the curse had a place to land (Prov. 26:2).

When we repent and ask for forgiveness, then there is nothing for the accuser to use against us before God. The devil has no more right to torment. The Bible tells us in 1 John 1:9 that if we confess our sins, He is faithful and just and will forgive all our sins – they have been removed, as the psalmist states in Psalm 103:12, *'As far as the east is from the west, so far has He removed our transgressions from us.'* The curses that land on us due to unrepented sins are removed when we repent and apply the blood of Jesus to them. We are told in Galatians 3:13 that we have been redeemed from the curse of the law by Jesus becoming a curse for us. Therefore, once repentance and forgiveness have been undertaken, we can declare that verse over our lives. We declare the finished work of Christ that the curse can no longer operate over our mind, body, spirit, possessions, or family; in fact over any part of our lives. The blood of Jesus has wiped out all the harmful effects of the curse.

While John was not completely healed after our time with Jack and Jean, we knew that a significant part of his healing had been done. The periods when he was at peace were increasing. He was sleeping longer, although he was still mostly withdrawn. But there was enough of a difference for John to keep fighting.

In prayer ministry, there is a term called 'walking out your healing'. It means that although all the spiritual aspects have been completed, the person has to now walk in new ways. They cannot go back to the old way of thinking and acting. The Bible states that we have to renew our minds (Rom. 12:2); we have to change, think differently. I always use the example of our thought patterns being like deep troughs that a tractor has ploughed to prepare the ground for the seeds. These thought patterns are highways that we have gone down for many, many years. We go down them automatically, without any conscious thinking. But now we must start thinking in a completely new direction, creating new thought patterns based on the truth of the word, and this takes effort and determination, until the new thought patterns become automatic, and the old ones disappear. In the last decade, we have heard about brain plasticity; our brain can regenerate itself and establish healthier pathways. According to Dr Caroline Leaf, establishing new neurological pathways is most difficult in the first four days but, within seven days, these new pathways start to become established and eventually, with repetition, become the 'norm'.[1]

John now had to use his mental muscles to create new thought patterns. Every time his thoughts wandered down the old negative, fearful patterns he would pull them back and, using 2 Timothy 1:7, would declare that he did not have a spirit of fear. I have to admire John, because it was not easy as he struggled and fought against negative thoughts. Often he would repeat the verse over and over again until he was clear from the enemy's attack.

Our time in Birmingham was a breakthrough for John in the area of fear, but we knew that recovery is never even, and there would be hiccups on the way.

One such occasion was when we returned home from going out, John went straight up to the bedroom. After a

---

1. https://drleaf.com

while, when he did not come down, I went up to see why. I found him lying in bed with the covers over his head, curtains closed, and the room in total darkness. The minute I entered the room, I could smell the spirit of fear. I rebuked the spirit commanding it to leave the room. I then shouted at John, 'Get up! I will not have a husband of the bedroom. What are you doing giving in to fear? Get downstairs!'

John was so shocked that he quickly got out of bed and went downstairs. Zero tolerance is what we are called to have for demonic spirits; we can never accept them, or make any agreements with them.

For both of us, the road we had chosen was very hard. For me, life during those times was like living continuously in a pressure cooker. I felt pressed and hemmed in from all sides. I often felt like I was suffocating; I did not seem to be able to breathe. One day I was home before John, and remember going around dazed in our kitchen/lounge area touching things, struggling for breath. The Lord's Prayer came to mind, and I found myself shouting out to God, 'Father in heaven? I don't want a father in heaven; I want a father here on earth. Where are you? Why aren't you here?'

Many a time I would just cry or shout before the Lord, depending on how John was. I suppose it was a release from all the emotions I was feeling. There were times that I would press into the scriptures, and hold on to the promises of his healing; other times I would just hurl questions at the Lord. I was not handling my emotions very well during John's illness. I would like to say that I came before the Lord and poured out how I was feeling, receiving peace and calmness from the Lord, but I did not. Deep down I was angry at John and the Lord. It was mainly anger and fear that kept me going. Most of the time I was on autopilot but, at the same time, I would not allow myself to even contemplate for a second that John would not be healed. Somewhere, really deep down, I had the conviction that the Lord was there, and we would be fine.

Similarly, I knew that while the Lord was shaking John, dealing with all the wrong foundations in his life, He was also shaking me. I realised that I had placed my security in John, our status, our good life, and money. Now with John's illness, I was confronted with the real possibility of losing everything. For John, being broken by the Lord, even though it was to build him up again, better and stronger, was very painful. Having to face things in his life that he had buried in his subconscious because they were too painful to look at and resolve, was excruciatingly difficult for him and us.

As life went on and we progressed, God was dealing with more issues. Another major issue was the loss of our third child under painful circumstances. John was fearful that by being intimate with me, I would get pregnant. It was an irrational fear: he had a vasectomy after we lost our third child, and I was passed that stage of life. The enemy tormented him, creating a tremendous conflict. He would reach out to me, then push me aside, only to reach out to me again. I could see the battle in him; sometimes he would win, and sometimes the fear would win. Some nights, as I lay next to him, I could sense the tension and the conflict in him and I would leave to sleep in a different bedroom. The enemy was having a 'field day', trying to destroy our marriage by creating such havoc in John, that he started seeing me as the cause of his problems. It led him to think that life was too hard and, if he left me and lived on the streets without any responsibility, then he would be at peace and I also would be free.

He would often say to me, with torment in his eyes, 'Let me go and just live on the streets. It's too hard here.'

Sometimes I would say, 'Don't be silly.' But there were a few times, when I had had enough, I would say, 'Go then.' Then he would look at the pain in my eyes and stay.

One evening, John and Helen invited us to their church because a prophet was coming to speak. I do not remember his name; all I remember was that his day job was working for the post office. He spoke about the love of the Lord and trusting in Him. I remember he used an example from his own family, how his young son would stand at the top of the stairs, with him at the bottom. Then his son would leap off the top step, flying into his father's waiting arms. This prophet said that we need to have such trust in our heavenly Father, to have absolute trust that, in whatever happens, he will catch us. After he spoke, he invited people to come forward for prayer. By now, wherever we went, if the opportunity to receive prayer was given, we went forward. While this man of God walked along the line of people receiving prayer, he had words of encouragement or specific words for them, which he spoke out loud. However, when it came to my turn, he whispered in my ear and what he said made me fly backward.

I landed on my back on the floor. The prophet said that the Lord would restore the intimacy in my marriage. I had not told anyone about John's battles in that area, or the lack of intimacy in our marriage. On hearing that, I sobbed and sobbed; I lay on the floor sobbing uncontrollably. The prophet had moved on, but he stopped, looked back at me on the floor, and said in an authoritative voice, as he begun to prophesy, 'No more crying, stop your crying.'

He went further, 'Others will call you blessed of women.'

He spoke much more, but I cannot remember the words. I did write his prophecy down and for many years had it in the drawer near my bed, but lost it when we moved countries. I *strongly* regret losing that piece of paper. I knew that the Lord had not given up on us, which reassured me.

There are many other instances of prayers and healings by the Lord on our journey that I could write about, but suffice to say that we were progressing on a bumpy road. One night in November, things came to a head. It started like any other night: we came home from work, had dinner, watched some television and then got ready for bed. But John was more agitated than ever. Usually we would go to bed, read our Bibles and go to sleep, but John could not settle. He started walking around the house, muttering to himself. It was the first time, throughout his illness, that I would actually say he was out of his mind. I could not seem to reach him and began to be fearful. It was now late, about 10.00 p.m., but I still rang Helen. I told her that I could not do this any longer, that I could not help him, and that I was going to call the hospital and have him Sectioned.

'No,' she said very firmly, almost shouting, 'don't do that. Ring Ben and Gill,' who had moved to the West Country. 'Go and see them,' she said.

I am so thankful to the Lord for Helen. Without her faith, encouragement and support, especially that night, I believe our ending would have been so very different. How we all need to have godly, faithful people around us. Reassured, but still shaking, I rang Gill immediately.

'Gill, it's Rita,' I said shakily, as she answered the phone. 'John is so bad, he is wandering around the house in a totally bemused state, almost like a trance. I can't seem to get through to him. He will not sit down, or go to bed. It is like he has completely lost his mind. I do not know what to do. Can we come and see you and Ben?'

Without hesitation she said, 'Of course,' and it was agreed that we would drive down the next day after work. She also prayed for me on the phone.

While all this was happening, I could see John walking around the house in a daze, mentally in a completely different place. I am sure that Gill and Ben prayed for us because, a little while later, I finally got through to him and said that tomorrow we would be going down to see Ben and Gill, and that now we needed to rest. From then on, he slowly quietened down, although neither of us got much sleep that night.

Early in the morning, I rang our friends who always looked after Socs for us while we were away, and made arrangements for them to have him. Then I rang Hilda, and told her what we were doing. She knew Ben and Gill too, and I wanted her to make sure that John left work early enough for our trip to the West Country. Now all I had to do was to get some time off work at short notice; would my manager agree?

When my manager came in, I asked to take some holiday leave for the next few days. We had friends in the West Country that we would like to go and see. Thank God, he agreed and so, skipping lunch, I left early. Meanwhile, Hilda had called me to say that while she was praying for us, Numbers 35:33 had come to mind, but she was not sure why. I filed it in the back of my mind.

I felt safe and comforted being with Ben and Gill. They had been so faithful as spiritual father and mother to us throughout our entire journey. They explained that a friend was going to pray with us who would not be free until the second night so for the first day we just rested, watched godly movies and talked. Ben had to go to work during the day, and John decided to go for a walk. I was apprehensive in case he did not come back, but Gill reassured me to let him go.

Ben and Gill had decided that they would fast until after we had prayed, although John and I did not. John did not even notice that he and I were the only ones eating. When their friend came around on the second night, we began to seek the Lord. While we were waiting on the Lord, the verses that Hilda mentioned came to mind, and I was prompted to share Numbers 35:33, which reads: *'So you shall not pollute the land where you are; for blood defiles the land, and no atonement can be made for the land, for the blood that is shed on it, except by the blood of him who shed it.'*

We all prayed further as we were not sure what, if anything, the Lord was showing us through this verse. John was quiet, trying to focus on what was happening. As we were praying, what came to my mind was our third child, and the copper intrauterine device (IUD) I was using at the time, as a contraceptive. Usually I would only share intimate things with women. In the room, apart from John, were two other men, one of whom I had never met before. But I knew how important this time was, so I shared about the IUD device I had been using, and Gill knew immediately the connection between the verse and what I shared. The copper IUD prevents the sperm from fertilising the egg and, in the rare cases where fertilisation does occur, it also prevents the implantation of the egg in the uterus, consequently aborting it. If we take the view that the beginning of life is at the fertilisation stage, then innocent blood is being shed each time a fertilised egg is aborted.

It became apparent to us, as a personal revelation, that through our ignorance we had shed innocent blood by using the IUD. It gave the enemy legal right to accuse us before the throne of God – we were guilty as charged. Even though it was done in ignorance, we were still responsible.

Although the verse states that the shedding of innocent blood can only be atoned for by the blood of the person who shed it, John and I could be saved from punishment because Jesus took the punishment on the cross for us. We just needed to repent and ask forgiveness. Ben and Gill then took us through a prayer of repentance for what we had done. At the same time, they came against the spirit of death and murder that would have entered through this door. Finally, by using the blood of Jesus, they asked the Lord to cleanse and heal us in every area of our lives.

Now at this point I suspect some people would roll their eyes, or put the book down, regarding this as too far-fetched. How can a verse from a book written thousands of years ago be relevant in the twenty-first century? We are told in Jeremiah 33:25 that the laws of heaven and earth are established. For example, the law of gravity has been in place since the creation of the world and now, in the twenty-first century, if you jump out of a window, you will still fall whether you believe the law or not. Time has not altered the law of gravity. It is the same with the laws of heaven, or God's spiritual laws. They are still in place and relevant.

Later on, as we progressed in our ministry, John and I began to understand how abhorrent to God the shedding of innocent blood is. Throughout the Bible, starting from Genesis 4:10 where God states that Abel's blood was crying out to Him, through to Revelation, where God will avenge the blood of His saints. The blood of an innocent man has to be accounted for. We read in Proverbs 6:16–17 that God hates the person who sheds innocent blood. The Hebrew word for 'hate' used here is 'sânê' which means 'to hate violently'. We did not understand how it all fitted together, but we knew that the push for John to kill himself, his fear of death, and the fear of me being pregnant, were somehow linked to the shedding of innocent blood. I know some people do not take the view that the beginning of life is at the fertilisation stage, and therefore there was no shedding of blood but, for all of us present at that time, it was evident that this was what the Lord was saying to us. Prayer ministry is often untidy. We cannot always adequately explain how things tie up; sometimes we just have to take it by faith and trust what the Lord is showing. Sometimes only time will show whether what has been prayed has hit the mark.

In our case, we knew that what was prayed with Ben and Gill had hit the mark and it was the turning point for John. We knew that we had reached the bottom and now we were on the way up. From the beginning of his illness in August until November, John had been spiralling downwards. After that time in the West Country, he was on an upward trajectory. Often there is a time lag between what occurs in the spiritual world and its manifestation in the physical world, so there was not an immediate change in John. In the days, weeks and months after the ministry in the West Country, John was improving; periods of sleep were increasing, he was eating more, he had longer times of engaging with me and others and, just as the man of God had said, our intimacy was restored. John had no more fear of me becoming pregnant; no longer a desire to push me away, to leave, or suicidal thoughts. The legal right of the accuser to harass us, to rob us, and to kill us, was taken away.

In January 1999 we received a pointer to a path that led us to John's complete healing, and had a most significant impact on us as a family.

Hilda was listening to an interview on Christian radio with a lady called Marion Daniel. Marion headed a healing and wholeness ministry called Sozo Ministries International, based in Romsey in Hampshire. Hilda was so impressed that she ordered a series of tapes (no CDs then) on 'The Foundation of Wholeness'. Once she had listened to them, she gave them to us. We also were inspired and encouraged by the teaching on the tapes. Marion's words were indeed anointed; John used to play them continually at night, which helped him to sleep soundly.

One Saturday night I was looking at the Sozo Ministries website and learned that they met every three weeks, at a school in Romsey, and that there was a meeting the very next day, Sunday, 14th February 1999 at 2.30 p.m.

Casually, I mentioned it to John and jokingly said, 'Shall we go?'

To my amazement, he said, 'Yes!' It was the best decision he ever made.

We arrived early at the school, around 2.00 p.m., and parked the car. Many people coming into the hall were carrying picnic baskets, which surprised us. At 2.30 p.m. we entered and were immediately struck by the presence and anointing of the Lord. It was like nothing we had experienced before; so wonderful, a balm to our spirits. There were about 250 people there, including children. The afternoon began with worship for the first hour, and then Marion spoke, after which people were invited to go up for prayer. Then everything stopped for tea – hence the picnic baskets. Fortunately for us, food and drink could be purchased. Lastly, there was an opportunity for further individual, private ministry if people wanted.

When the invitation was given to go up for prayer, we responded. By the time Marion came to pray for us, we were both in tears, as the Holy Spirit was touching us. John decided that he would like to have further ministry. We registered our names, and bought some food to eat; they sell the best carrot cake I have ever tasted. We sat down to wait for the ministry sessions to begin and Marion came over to us. She asked if we were in leadership or ministry, as she had a heart to minister to those people. We said that we were, at one time, in that position and explained what had happened to us with John's illness. She was so warm and loving, listening intently. When she realised that we were going to have further ministry, she went and checked out who was being allocated to us, and then changed counsellors to two people that she said would be more suited.

We met with these two amazing women who, after listening to our story, knew exactly what to pray. They took us to Revelation 9:11: *'And they had as king over them the angel of the bottomless pit, whose name in Hebrew is Abaddon, but in Greek he has the name Apollyon.'*

They explained that these words, Abaddon and Apollyon, mean 'the Destroyer' and that this demon was at work in John's life. As they spoke, we could identify that the enemy had indeed been trying to destroy our family, and us. They came against this spirit, rebuked it and cast it out. We knew that something had significantly shifted in us, and the enemy had lost ground. On the long journey home, we felt so free and full of hope, compared to when we went there.

From that time on, we were regular visitors to Sozo Ministries down in Romsey. It became our spiritual home, and we became fellow labourers in the ministry, part of the team, helping in any way we could. Our boys also attended when they could and, for a couple of years, our son Mark became their worship leader. This ministry with our spiritual brothers and sisters has had a most significant impact on our family. Even though we reside in Australia, currently leading our own ministry, Sozo Ministries is always our first port of call when we need serious help or advice. We are privileged that Marion and her family are very special friends, and we will always keep in touch, and try to visit them when we are in England.

Sozo Ministries International held conferences regarding specific areas of ministry. One such area was 'Freedom from Freemasonry', and Marion suggested that we should attend. Pondering this suggestion, we thought there was no known Freemasonry in either of our backgrounds, especially as we came from the Middle East. In John's ancestry, going back many generations, they were all Christians. In my history, as there was a mixture of Islam and Christianity, it was highly unlikely there would be any Masons. However, we took her advice and attended the conference.

It was a residential conference, running from Friday night to Sunday afternoon, with over 100 people attending. On Friday night, Marion spoke on Deuteronomy 18:9–14, about the forbidden practices of the occult, and took us through corporate ministry in preparation for the next day. All day Saturday, Alan Daniel (Marion's brother) took us through renouncing all of the thirty-three steps of Freemasonry.

Saturday was very intense. Even though we stopped for lunch, it was hard going. Corporately we repeated after Alan all the renunciations, and at specific points Alan would stop and break the curses he felt were still operating over us. John, through gritted teeth, got through the day. At one point, I could feel the anger and battle in John. I moved away to the back of the room, not feeling safe being next to John, and left him to Alan and the Lord. However, John got through the day even though he was so tired by the end of it.

Alan came up to me at the end of Saturday and said, 'I could see the huge struggle that John was going through repeating the renunciations. Bless him. You know I would have done it all just for him.'

That night was a free evening of worship which was balm to our souls and refreshed us.

We had come to the conference in pure faith and trust in Marion's discernment, even though we could not see how it would be relevant. But the next morning we knew precisely how appropriate it was. The first thing John said, with wonder in his voice, when he awoke was, 'For the first time in my life, my mind is at peace.'

I could see the change in his face, especially in his eyes. He was completely healed, instantly, and miraculously.

To this day we do not know what renouncing all the thirty-three steps of Freemasonry had to do with his healing. The only explanation we came to was that, at the beginning of Saturday, we were shown a DVD of an ex-Mason speaking about Freemasonry, and another person who had been involved in witchcraft, explaining that craft. To our amazement, there was no difference. All of us have paganism and witchcraft in our family lines, and John was no exception. Maybe the breaking of some of the curses that Alan undertook was relevant to John and his bloodline, we do not know. As we state in prayer ministry, it's difficult to draw straight lines and tie-up everything neatly. The only thing we can attest is that after that conference John was healed completely and he has never looked back.

By the summer of 1999 John was back entirely: running the business and looking at new ways to improve it. Mark was working there too, helping his dad. David was in Mexico on holiday. I had left work and was planning to go into full-time study, to get my degree in Christian and Religious Studies in September. I was enjoying the summer.

One day I decided to paint our summer house – the wood needed a lift, and I could not remember when it last had loving attention. Having not done such a task previously, I remember brushing away, enjoying the sun on my face, listening to the birds and watching Socs snoozing on the grass. Suddenly I collapsed in tears on the floor, paint brush still in hand. The lid of the pressure cooker that I had lived under for a long time flipped off, and I just sobbed and sobbed. I cried from sheer relief, thankfulness and joy. I wept before the Lord, and poured out my gratefulness to Him for all He had done. I did not know then that the past year of working at such deep foundational level, for both John and I, was the Lord preparing us for the next stage of our lives, for the building of us, and our ministry. All I knew was that, suddenly, the world had never looked more beautiful and our lives were back to normal.

CHAPTER NINE

REFLECTIONS

John

It is interesting to read the last three chapters of Rita's recollection of what ensued throughout my breakdown, as my memory is somewhat scant of particular events. What I do remember is that, the day I snapped, we were away on holiday and it was as if I suddenly found myself in a nightmare, with an excruciating pain in my head that would not go away. The pain in my head was so severe at times that I contemplated suicide. Voices in my head were telling me that I was worthless, useless, and my entire life was a sham. The voices felt like a broken record player stuck in one spot, going round and round, repeating the same thing all day long, giving me no rest. I had no hope and the thought of committing suicide seemed the only way out of this mess. I did not necessarily want to kill myself, but I did not know how else to get rid of the pain in my head. The suicidal thoughts came in waves and, at the height of my breakdown, it was a daily fight against the continuous voices in my head that told me all I had to do was take the car and drive it into a wall.

Initially, each day seemed the same without any respite. Having slept for only a few hours, or not at all, I would get up very early in the morning, hoping the pain would stop. Each day seemed to go on forever, with the pain in my head coming in waves like the sea lapping against the sand. The sense of hopelessness was there, and I could not see any sign of light at the end of a dark tunnel. I was so consumed in my own world that I could not participate in any other function pertaining to daily living.

As I mentioned, my recollection of my breakdown is vague, but I do have a few memories. Now that I am healed because of the work that Jesus accomplished in my life, I can recollect events without being disturbed. I can face them, look at the scars and prod them, but they no longer cause me to react, have a hold on me, or drag me down.

The first thing I remember was not being able to sleep at night. Going to bed in itself was a battle, and something I dreaded. I knew that I would not be able to sleep; in fact, most nights, especially within the first few weeks of my breakdown, I would stay awake all night. Sometimes I would get extremely agitated and pace around the house till the sun came up. When I remained in bed, I would toss and turn and almost hope that, with the dawn, something different would happen, that this was all a bad nightmare. But then I would wake up and be my old self again. My usual hearty appetite for food disappeared at the same time, and everything tasted like cardboard. As a result, I lost a lot of weight and my clothes would drape loosely around my body.

When I was fourteen years old, I broke my right arm at school doing the high jump. I got immediate attention, everyone was kind to me, and people came and asked me if they could help. The ambulance arrived and, after an operation, I ended up with a cast on my arm. The reaction from everyone was so good. Friends wanted to sign the cast to express good wishes. In contrast, when I was forty-five years old, my head 'broke' and I was met with silence; people around me, including the church we belonged to, did not know what to do or say.

At the time of my breakdown we were members of our local Baptist church, and I was on the leadership team. As a team, we had many challenges ahead, and when I rang one of my fellow deacons to explain what was happening to me, my perception was that he was more concerned that I was absenting myself from the work we had to undertake, than how I was. There was neither understanding nor sympathy for my predicament. I don't say that with any bitterness, nor do I blame those who felt they did not know what to say, or how to respond to our needs. Even today, mental health issues still carry a stigma.

I was aware that our lives had gone from a busy, vibrant, social and church life, to almost isolation. Rita, I knew, kept us away from people who would not understand the journey we were on, or who would not understand how to deal with me. At the same time, I was withdrawing from people, often morose and quiet, lost in my little world. The devil's scheme is to isolate people through the lie that what they are going through cannot be shared with others. It can be shared, but ask God first who to share it with, and He will direct you to the people who can at least listen with compassion. The most unhelpful individuals, I found, were well-meaning friends, unable just to listen, who had a preconceived mantra, telling us how we could fix things.

During that time, it was God's provision that both the boys were away at university, enabling Rita to be able to use David's bedroom to get a few hours of sleep, and then get up and go to work. To this day, I do not know how she coped. She must have battled with her doubts and fears and struggled, on top of that, to hold everything together. But her strong faith in Christ and believing that ultimately God would not forsake us, kept her going and for that I will be eternally grateful to her.

I was totally engulfed in fear; it was like being surrounded by fog. The fear was extremely debilitating.

I remember one day when Rita was out of the house, I was on my own and wanted to go for a walk in our local park. It was a beautiful, sunny day and as I got to the front door, this fear suddenly hit me. The voices in my head said that if I stepped out of the house something would hit me, like a boulder from the sky, and I would die. Today, as I write this, it sounds ridiculous but, at the time, the fear was very real to me. Apart from that, the devil was placing a magnifying glass over everything else out there that could be perceived as dangerous. Suddenly, it seemed crossing the road was fraught with dangers, and cars were like lions waiting to devour me. I must have stayed frozen at the front door for hours, until Rita came home.

'What are you doing?' she asked, as she saw me at the front door.

'I wanted to go out, but I am frightened,' I shakily replied.

'What are you frightened of?' she asked impatiently, looking around, trying to see what I was frightened of.

'There are dangers out there. Cars and people,' I stammered timidly.

'Oh, don't be so ridiculous,' she exclaimed as she stormed past me.

She was so angry, but I don't blame her one bit because at the time she was doing almost everything and under immense strain. When I did push through the fear (often at Rita's nagging) to go outside, I thought that everyone was looking at me, and judging me as a loser.

Rita would bully me into facing head-on the many irrational fears I had. This was tough love, and something I needed in order to get over my fears. She would always quote an acronym for fear which is, 'False Evidence Appearing Real'. I came to realise that, many times, the fears we have are perceived or imagined and, most times, when we face them head-on, we realise that we had nothing to be afraid of. Each time I was faced with fear I had the choice of whether to believe the fear, or the Lord.

At one significant point in my breakdown, I found myself wrestling with God and myself about the reality of who God was.

'God,' I cried out, 'either Your word is a lot of rubbish, full of myths and made-up stories, or totally true. Come on, show Yourself!'

In my darkest hour, I was no longer willing to compromise. Sitting on the fence was now a painful experience; I could feel a tug-of-war going on in my life. Either I was going to walk away from God, or experience Him in a totally new way. I could no longer mess with God. I struggled with that dilemma for a time, and then a deep sense of God's presence appeared in the room. I found myself face down on the ground, unable to stand because of His might and power. Instead of toying with Him, I had a deep sense of fear that I was in front of Almighty God. At that instant, I understood the enormity of the sacrifice He had made for me in allowing His only Son, Jesus, to be crucified for my sins. Then the realisation came to me that Jesus became the sacrificial lamb for me, so that I can enter the Father's presence and still be alive. That experience left me without any doubt; I could no longer compromise God's word and cherry-pick bits that I liked. It was then that I felt God say to me, 'Your latter days will be better than your former days.'

Then, a warm love engulfed me that I had never experienced before. It was a real experience, which I now write in humility, as I believe God was demonstrating His power and telling the enemy, 'This far and no more.'

During my breakdown, my relationship with Rita was sorely tested. Apart from being isolated from most of our friends, I was also distancing myself from Rita. For months there was a lack of physicality in our relationship as often I would withdraw from Rita, not even wanting a touch. It almost broke our marriage, but Rita's trust in God kept our union together. I cannot write much more about this part our life because of a lack of memory and awareness around that time. I am sure there is a lot more stuff to unpack, maybe another book could be *Christian Marriage Through Hardships*. However, I do remember that as I got better, the warmth towards my Rita returned, and we started 'dating' again.

I still marvel at Rita's tenacity, her capacity to keep going under extreme pressure, and her resilience in being able to bounce back from adversity. She was not going to let the enemy destroy everything we had, and for that I will always be grateful to her. Today I have a special closeness to my wife Rita, which I believe would not have been possible had we not gone through this experience.

I remember having a lot of prayers, not only from our good friends John and Helen but a few other friends linked to Wholeness Through Christ. Rita was adamant that anyone praying for me should have the same faith as she did, that God can touch, heal and renew completely, regardless of the severity of the illness. Some of the prayers were directed into the generational lines on both my mother's and father's sides of the family. The prayer times sometimes resulted in some form of spiritual deliverance from demonic forces.

I started using the word of God against the enemy. Each day, I would declare that the blood of the Lamb washed me clean, protected me totally, and cleansed me from all sin. I remember in the early days of my breakdown, Ben told me about the importance of using scripture to overcome the devil's grip on my life. I was very weak then, and I asked him how many times a day I had to declare scripture verses. His answer was, 'As many times as it takes for the devil to go away.'

On hearing this advice, I was initially disheartened. But as I started using God's word, I gradually gained strength. I found that repeating scripture over and over again became a delight, instead of a chore. As an example, when I was hearing voices in my head, gripping me in fear and telling me I would never get better, I started shouting back at the voices, sometimes as often as every few minutes: *'For God has not given us a spirit of fear, but of power and of love and of a sound mind'* (2 Tim. 1:7).

I started concentrating on the positive signs of progress, and began giving thanks to God for those good times. I learned to come to my heavenly Father, first with thanksgiving and praise, and then to bring my petitions before Him (Phil. 4:6).

Eventually, as a result of all the prayers I was receiving, along with using the scriptures, I slowly began to get better. It was like brief rays of sunlight penetrating my life, giving me drops of hope.

The support I got from Rita and some close friends, and the way God used them, was one of the major factors that helped my 'breakdown' result in a 'breakthrough'. I can categorically state that, without that support, I would be in a different situation today.

I remember one day, Rita took me down to our friends Ben and Gill, who lived in the West Country, to receive more prayer ministry. That time was so significant in my breakthrough.

The next morning, having slept well, I got up feeling unusually upbeat. I remember going out for a walk and enjoying the town's ancient picturesque buildings. Suddenly, without warning, voices emerged in my head, relentlessly telling me that I was a useless husband and father, and that the family would be much better off without me. The voices were prompting me just to carry on walking, and not return to Rita. I remember walking for miles and agreeing with the voices that this was a good idea. At that point, I was convinced Rita and the boys would be much better off without me. I'd often had similar thoughts about living on the streets, but was able to dismiss them. This time they seemed to overpower me.

Eventually, having walked for what seemed like an eternity, I stopped from sheer exhaustion. Where I rested, there was an isolated cottage in front of me. By now it must have been just after lunch, and I noticed through the window of the cottage an elderly man still in his pyjamas. He seemed alone and was looking aimlessly out of the window, marking time. Then a warm, gentle voice in my head said, 'Do you want to end up sad and lonely?' I remember immediately turning around to the destructive voices in my head telling them to, 'Get lost,' in a loud voice. Without realising it, I was starting to fight back, and not agreeing with everything the voices were telling me. I walked back to Rita and my friends after many hours, looking very dishevelled, I am sure.

Rita greeted me with, 'Nice walk, darling?' with no outward show of concern. When I was much better, Rita later told me that while I was away walking that morning, she and Gill were engaged in spiritual warfare, fighting for our family, and me, in prayer. They felt it was a breaking point, critical for the very survival of our family, which the devil was out to destroy. That night when they prayed for me, God touched me in a miraculous way; I felt a weight had lifted off my shoulders. Thanks to the power of prayer, this event was a major stepping stone on the road to recovery.

I have a few other memories of events which touched and delivered me. The most significant was the 'Freedom from Freemasonry Conference' that we attended. I struggled throughout the whole day. At times I just wanted to walk away, as I felt a tremendous battle ensuing within me. I found renouncing some of the Freemasonry oaths difficult, often saying them through clenched teeth. I remember someone prompting me to keep my eyes open and concentrate. By the end of the final day, I was so exhausted that I just managed to go to bed, and I slept soundly for eight to ten hours.

When I woke up next morning, my whole body felt like what I can only describe as a lump of jelly. It was a pleasant experience, as I felt no tension in my muscles, no anxiety, and a sense of calmness that I had never experienced before. My entire mind was still, and that was the strangest feeling of all. I was not restless, trying to work out the next thing, or thinking about the future. My mind was perfectly and beautifully still – something which I had never experienced before. A tremendous sense of calmness permeated my entire body. Something miraculous had happened, and I knew that I had reached the end of my long journey: I was totally healed.

I sometimes wonder why God did not touch me with a single prayer, and heal me instantly, instead of taking me through this journey. I do not doubt that God could do that, immediately heal someone in my state, because He is sovereign. But I am reminded of Exodus 23:29–30 where we are told how the Lord brought the Israelites into the Promised Land. We are told that the Lord would not drive out their enemies in the land in one go, because the land would become desolate and filled with wild animals; instead He would do so little by little, till they had increased enough to possess the land. In Luke 11:24–26, Jesus refers to this principle too, that if you clear an area and leave it empty, then the final condition of the person would be worse than the first. In my case, I believe the Lord wanted to work on me gradually. So that, in each area He dealt with, I would overcome the enemy, gain strength and be filled with the Holy Spirit. Thus I would become a better, spiritually stronger person, having no doubt in my mind that God and the spiritual dimension are real. God's plan for me was not just to restore my old self, but to change me completely, to what He always planned for me to be; free of all the emotional rubbish and sin that stood in the way of my relationship with Him.

I have often pondered the question, 'Could all of this have been prevented?' and reluctantly concluded that the answer is, 'Yes', for two main reasons.

The most important reason was that I was not living according to God's word. The Bible is the story of God's plan of salvation for all humanity. It tells us of God's love and how, through Jesus, we can be saved and healed. But it is also a book about preventive medicine. The creator God gives us instruction for living a godly and healthy life, and in how to prevent sickness and trouble in the first place. Not only was I not following the Maker's instructions, but I was not even reading them.

Many scriptures in the Bible instruct us how to live well. Below are a few that were relevant to my situation. The fifth commandment reads: *'Honour your father and mother so that you might live long in the land that the LORD your God is giving you'* (Exod. 20:12).

And Paul, in Ephesians 6:3, expands it more, stating that if we follow this commandment then things will go well with us, and we will enjoy long life on the earth. I had read or heard about that commandment often, but never fully believed or obeyed it. Many times I had dishonoured my parents, in my heart and deeds, and then wondered why things did not go well with me.

Proverbs 3:5–6 states, if we trust in the Lord (not ourselves), and lean into His understanding, not our own, acknowledging Him in all ways, then the Lord will make our paths straight. Verses 7 and 8 go on to say that if we fear the Lord and shun evil, this will bring health to our bodies, and nourishment to our bones. I did not follow this; on the contrary, I totally depended on my understanding, and did not fear or honour the Lord as He deserved.

Jeremiah 17:5 says that the man who depends on his flesh, who trusts in man, and whose heart turns away from the Lord, will be cursed. I did exactly that and came under that curse. If we want to come under blessings, then the Bible is very clear that obedience brings blessings, and disobedience brings curses (Deut. 28), a principle still relevant and in operation today.

Romans 8:6 (NIV) states: *'The mind governed by the flesh is death, but the mind governed by the Spirit is life and peace.'*

My mind was governed by me.

'You will keep him in perfect peace, whose mind is stayed on You, because he trusts in You' (Isaiah 26:3).

For most of my life, I trusted only in John Helvadjian.

'Great peace have those who love Your law, and nothing causes them to stumble' (Psalm 119:165).

Most of the time I did not even read His law, let alone love it.

'Cast your burden on the LORD, and He shall sustain you; He shall never permit the righteous to be moved' (Psalm 55:22).

In my pride and independence, I never cast my burdens on to the Lord.

Many scriptures tell us that we have to forgive: Colossians 3:13, Ephesians 4:32, Mark 11:25 and Matthew 6:12 are but a few. Others speak of the consequences of not forgiving; Matthew 6:14–15 tells us that if we do not forgive others then the Lord will not forgive us. By holding on to unforgiveness, I was positioning myself in a place where God would not forgive me. And the parable of the Unmerciful Servant in Matthew18:21–35 tells us that if we do not forgive, then Father God will treat us the same way as the master did his unmerciful servant; he sent him to the jailers to be tortured. Again, I did not follow God's word and, due to my unforgiving heart, I was being tormented.

These are a few scriptures to illustrate how the word directs us, and helps us to live well – scriptures that I did not heed.

Furthermore, James 1:25 (NIV) states: *'Whoever looks intently into the perfect law that gives freedom, and continues in it – not forgetting what they have heard, but doing it – they will be blessed in what they do.'*

But I was doing the exact opposite, as James 1:23–24 (NIV) says: *'Anyone who listens to the word but does not do what it says is like someone who looks at his face in a mirror and, after looking at himself, goes away and immediately forgets what he looks like.'*

You may say that I am too hard on myself, that it is nigh on impossible to live a hundred per cent according to God's word; we are human after all. I would agree, but all the Lord is looking for is a heart willing to live according to His word and He has given us the Holy Spirit to help us.

'As His divine power has given to us all things that pertain to life and godliness, through the knowledge of Him who called us by glory and virtue' (2 Peter 1:3).

The second reason why I believe that my illness could have been prevented was that I did not heed the warnings. The Lord had sent so many messengers to me, to warn me of the dangerous path I was on. Friends, with gentle comments like: 'John, do you think that you are working too hard? Should you take a break or relax a little?' or 'You don't seem OK; is everything alright?'

Many opportunities came when I attended Wholeness Through Christ to deal with my own and generational issues. I could have made so much more of the opportunities that I was given. I remember once leaving early, with the attitude that I was OK and had no need to stay further.

Then there was Rita with her challenging questions: 'Where was I at in my walk with the Lord?' or 'When was the last time you read the word or spent time with Father God?'

My dad tried to advise me to have a kinder, gentler attitude to life.

But most of all, there were warnings through the gentle voice of the Holy Spirit, the niggling disquiet in my spirit that I squashed so many times.

All these and many others were, I believe, sent by the Lord as warnings, gentle corrections to the path I was on. I am ashamed to say that, in the pride and stubbornness of my heart, I did not listen.

I did not deal with all my fears at the same time. In January 2012, almost thirteen years after my breakthrough, in order to finally face my fear and dislike of everything medical, I volunteered as a helper in the palliative ward of Greenwich Hospital in Sydney, where we live. I talked to patients and their families, being available for them. I witnessed a young man, who was only thirty-five years old, dying of terminal cancer while his mother held his hand with tears in her eyes. This was one of the hardest things I did, ultimately facing my biggest fear: death. I now have the greatest respect for all the medical staff in that hospital, and value the expertise that doctors can bring to the care of patients. For all of us, there will be new situations in which we have to face fears. It is part of life; the question is, do we face them, or allow them to paralyse us?

In my impatience, I learned patience as I waited on God for His perfect way of healing me and His perfect timing in that process. God was teaching me multiple lessons at the same time; I started thanking God not only for the big things, but also giving Him thanks for the small things. I know now that God is interested in all aspects of my life and wants a relationship with me where I can totally confide in Him. I wake up every day and thank my heavenly Father for the very breath that I take.

In my experience, recovery was not a linear process but one fraught with ups and downs. As I progressed, and gained strength, there were more ups than downs. I found that relapse was also part of my journey. When it happened, I knew not to fear that I was going to be ill again. We learned that if we could work out when, how and why the relapse happened, the information helped in returning to God in prayer for further healing.

I can now see clearly why God had to rescue me in such a dramatic, but perfect, way. He was answering my prayers, even if they were from a half-hearted desire to progress in my spiritual life. I was trying to serve two masters, and wanted the best of both worlds. But God would not allow that to happen. He is a jealous God unwilling to share His position in my life with anyone, or anything.

I am now very comfortable in my own skin having the full knowledge that God made me beautifully and wonderfully in His own image (Ps. 139:14). He loves me with an everlasting love (Jer. 31:3). As a result, I now see God as my heavenly Father who desires the best for me: not my best, but His. I often feel His love tangibly, an experience like having a warm, comfortable blanket draped around me.

We have nearly come to the end of our story, but I want to reiterate that the devil will try to use our mind as his point of entry. That's why fixing our eyes on Jesus, and having our minds renewed daily, will not give the enemy room to get in. That's why the Bible says in Ephesians 4:22–23 *'that you put off, concerning your former conduct, the old man which grows corrupt according to the deceitful lusts, and be renewed in the spirit of your mind'*.

Having our minds regularly refreshed and renewed by the power of the Holy Spirit is our responsibility, instead of having our minds corrupted by what we think and see. The Bible also instructs us to guard our words, not letting any corrupt words come out of our mouths but only such as is good for building up, as fits the occasion, that it may give grace to those who hear (Eph. 4:29).

Now I am a different man to the one I was before my breakthrough. But I am still a work in progress. As 2

Corinthians 3:18 states: *'But we all, with unveiled face, beholding as in a mirror the glory of the Lord, are being transformed into the same image from glory to glory, just as by the Spirit of the Lord.'*

God is refining me, and always will continue to refine and change me, for I am not yet completely transformed into His Son's image.

I am now a psychotherapist and Clinical Supervisor and work in my own private practice. I treat individuals and couples who are going through rough times mentally, physically and spiritually. I am often asked if there is a conflict between my being psychologically trained and having the Christian faith. To that I answer, 'No.' I maintain that the work I do is 80 per cent life experience and 20 per cent academic study. I am totally dependent on God to provide direction and discernment. As a psychotherapist with Christian beliefs, when working with non-Christian clients, I use modalities learned in my profession. And while I am using those modalities, I am silently praying that God will touch them. For I know that Jesus is the only one who can save and transform lives. With Christian clients, and especially those who allow me to pray for them, I pull out all the stops, and pray with authority in accordance with the word of God. I can categorically state that the word of God, the shed blood of Jesus, and the power of the Holy Spirit set us free. My trust and belief are in the word of God, not psychology.

Through this experience we have learned some profound lessons:

- 'Do not mess with God' because He is real. God is bigger and mightier than we can ever imagine or contemplate. He spoke and the universe was created and the Bible states that He holds all of that in the palm of His hand (Isa. 40:12).

- The Bible is the true and the only word of God, and should not be altered or compromised. It is powerful and needs to be used as a sword. Use the word of God against the enemy.

- The devil is real. He has his host of fallen angels and demons, which he controls and directs. My experience has left me in no doubt that all this is real and that there is a battle in the heavenly dimension for our lives.

- God's desire is for each one of His children to be whole and has made provision for this through the finished work of the cross.

- We cannot put God in our convenient box, getting Him out like a 'genie in a bottle' whenever we feel like it, or need Him to fix things, putting Him back when things are going well for us.

- God really does answer prayer, even when we our prayers are half-hearted, or if we are singing them as hymns or songs. When Rita and I prayed that morning in January 1998, 'God, take us on in our lives at any cost,' my desire was to appease Rita, not thinking that God would answer our prayers in His own way, and in His own time.

- When receiving prayer, or praying for someone else, especially with another person, there needs to be unity in believing that God can bring perfect healing. The unity and combined prayers of saints can have a more powerful impact when that faith is undivided, and applied in prayer. There is power when two or more come together, agree on what God is showing them, and then pray it through.

- It is important to face one's fears. Having fear, instead of faith, means we are choosing to believe the lies of the devil, rather than the word of the Lord.

- It is important to deal with issues or sins promptly. They never disappear by being ignored; they just go deeper and fester. Time is not a healer.

- To apply the blood of Christ. Whenever I felt under attack I would declare the blood of Jesus over me. The enemy has then to flee because the shed blood of Jesus Christ on the cross is the most powerful substance to have hit planet earth.

- Seize all negative, lying thoughts immediately, without entertaining them, taking *'captive every thought to make it obedient to Christ'* (2 Cor. 10:5 NIV). Every time I did so helped God's word to penetrate my heart with the truth. Eventually, God's word slowly dispelled the devil's lies and, with continuous declaration of His powerful word, strength and sanity returned to me.

But the most important lesson we have learnt is the love of the Father. Even though there were times when it was so dark and He seemed so far away, He was there. When we dug in deep, when we were at rock bottom, when we cried out to Him in despair, we felt His love. When we felt we could go on no further He encouraged us, either by speaking to us directly, or by His written word, or through the godly people He gave us. We knew we were much loved by our heavenly Father. We are His children and, as children, there are times when we need to be disciplined for our own good.

I cannot imagine where we would be now if our Father had not lovingly intervened, and brought us back to Him. We are so grateful to Him for this.

Rita and I started our journey of spiritual healing in 1990 and, out of all our experiences and lessons learned, we have been used by our Lord to minister to the Body of Christ. We have, by the grace of God, seen many amazing works of the Lord, bringing God's love, hope and healing to others in the Body of Christ. It is an amazing privilege but an awesome responsibility.

We found writing this book extremely challenging. There were times we questioned why we were doing this. To become famous as an author, write a best seller, make lots of money, or get well known? We wondered what people would say if they knew the real truth about us. Would they think less of us? Maybe we should have kept back some of the intimate details of the story to make it more palatable? These were the questions buzzing in our heads as we grappled with this book. From the beginning, though, we felt that this story was God-directed, and that we were to be obedient in writing it. Consequently, all other questions became totally secondary.

We believe that God wants our story told so that our brothers and sisters in Christ, who might be going through similar troubles, will be encouraged, have hope, and know that God is the answer to all their problems, however large or small. Through the suffering of Jesus, we can all be healed and transformed.

APPENDIX I
Resources

Ministries

Our contact details are:

Complete Ministries International
Email: completeministries.i@gmail.com
Web: www.completeministriesinternational.com
Tel: +61 (0) 2 94281279

Jubilee Resources International Inc.
PO Box 36-044,
Wellington Mail Centre 5045,
New Zealand
Tel: +64-4-939-1910
Fax: +64-4-939-1911
Email: info@jubileeresources.org
Web: www.jubileeresources.org

Sozo Ministries International
Dunwood Oaks,
Danes Road,
Awbridge,
Hampshire
SO51 0GF
England
Tel: +44 (0)1794 344920
Email: email@sozo.org
Web: www.sozo.org

Resources

Has Anyone Seen My Father?
Author: Marion Daniel
Publisher: New Wine Press, 2008
Available from Sozo Ministries International

What Am I Worth?
Author: Marion Daniel
Publisher: New Wine Press, 2010
Available from Sozo Ministries International

Blessing or Curse: You Can Choose
Author: Derek Prince
Publisher: Derek Prince Ministries, 2007

Prayers and Proclamations
Author: Derek Prince
Publisher: Whitaker House, 2010

How to Apply the Blood
Author: Derek Prince
https://www.dpmuk.org/product/how-to-apply-the-blood

Living Free in Christ
Author: Neil Anderson
Publisher: Gospel Light Publications, 1993

Freedom From Fear
Authors: Neil Anderson & Rich Miller
Publisher: Monarch Books, 2007

Unmasking Freemasonry
Author: Selwyn Stevens
Publisher: Jubilee Resources, 2004

Ministry Prayers that Liberate
Author: Selwyn Stevens
Publisher: Jubilee Resources, 2014
(Visit his website www.jubileeresources.org for more of his books)

Scripture Keys for Kingdom Living
Author: June Newman Davis
Publisher: Scripture Keys Ministries, 2006
Available from Sozo Ministries International

APPENDIX II
Prayers

These prayers are a guide only. Please be led by the Holy Spirit.

If you have never accepted the Lord Jesus into your life, now is the time!
Today I acknowledge God the Father, Jesus the Son and the Holy Spirit; God in three persons.

Lord God, I come to You as a sinner. I acknowledge that You sent Your Son, the Lord Jesus Christ, to take my punishment on the cross. Jesus died and rose again on the third day so that I can become a child of Yours and have eternal life. Therefore, I come to You and repent and ask Your forgiveness for my sins.

Thank You that Jesus shed His blood for the forgiveness of my sins that I can come into relationship with You, Father God. And I ask to be born again of the spirit of God.

I surrender my life and will to You, Lord Jesus, and invite You to come into my life by Your Holy Spirit, and I acknowledge You as my Lord and Saviour. I choose this day to turn from my old way of life, not looking back but moving forward with You.

I invite You, Holy Spirit, to come in and fill me to overflowing with Your presence. I ask that You may walk with me, convicting me of sin and revealing Jesus to me.

Thank You, Father God, that I am now a child of Yours, adopted into Your family and co-heirs with Christ.

In Jesus' name. Amen.

Welcome to The Family! We would encourage you to find a body of believers that function as the early church did in Acts: Bible based, full of worship and power.

Try to talk to your heavenly Father as often as you can. He always has an ear for you! And for daily food, read God's word.

Prayer for release from un-forgiveness

Father God, Your word states that I need to forgive as You have forgiven me (Matthew 18:21–35).

So, Father God, I choose to forgive *[person's/organisational name]* for *[state what they have done]*.

Father God, I come before You and ask Your forgiveness for harbouring unforgiveness against *[insert name or organisation here]*. I also ask Your forgiveness for all resentment, hatred, grudges and bitterness that I held against *[person's name/ organisation name]*.

I repent, renounce and ask Your forgiveness for all the thoughts, words and deeds that I have undertaken against *[person's/organisation name]* and declare them now to be of no effect over their mind, body and spirit.

I repent, renounce and break any curses that I may have spoken or thought against them *[if the Holy Spirit brings to mind anything specific, mention it here]* and declare those curses to not affect their mind, body and spirit.

I repent and renounce of any spoken or unspoken vows that I may have made against *[person's/organisational name, if the Holy Spirit brings to mind anything specific, mention it here]* and declare them to not affect their mind, body and spirit and myself.

I choose to release *[person's/organisational name]* from all my un-forgiveness, resentment, hatred, grudges and bitterness.

I ask that You cleanse me by Your precious Son's blood from all defilement that may have been caused by these sins.

Father God, I ask that You bless them abundantly in all areas of their lives, physically, spiritually and mentally.

In Jesus' name, I come against every negative thought, word and deed directed against me by *[person's/organisation name]* and declare them not to affect my mind, body and spirit. In Jesus' name, I break any curses directed against me, because Your word says that Jesus became a curse on the tree for me.

Father God, I ask that You heal me from all the hurts and wounds that have been inflicted on my mind, body and spirit because of *[person/organisational name]*.

In Jesus' name. Amen.

Prayer for release from generational sins
Leviticus 26:40–41, Daniel 9:1–19

Father God, I stand in the gap of my forefathers and confess and renounce *[state here what specifically you are identifying that needs confessing e.g. fear, pride, lust, idolatry]* take accountability for the sins of my forefathers through my generational bloodlines up to the four and tenth generation.

According to Your word we have broken Your *[state which commandment has been broken or any other sin]* and I confess on behalf of my forefathers *[and, if applicable, repent for yourself]*.

In the name of Jesus, on behalf of my forefathers I break every agreement that was made, whether spoken, unspoken or written, with the evil one in the spiritual realm. I declare that all these agreements to be null and void over my mind, body and spirit and all my family, and have been superseded by my agreement with the Lord Jesus Christ.

In Jesus' mighty name I break every agreement that was made by my forefathers with the spirit of *[state here which spirit is linked with the sin you are confessing, e.g. if fear then a spirit of fear, etc.]*, whether spoken, unspoken or written in the spiritual realm. I now declare this agreement to be null and void over my life and family. This agreement has been superseded by my agreement with Jesus, who is Lord over my life.

Holy Spirit, I ask that You come now and fill me in all areas where the enemy has affected me.

Father God, 1 Peter 1:18–19 states that I have been redeemed by the empty ways of my forefathers with the precious blood of Jesus so, in Jesus' name, I declare now I am redeemed from my forefathers and now am part of God's family and from the bloodline of Jesus Christ.

In Jesus' name. Amen.

Prayer for healing from bereavement/grief

Father, the God of all comfort (2 Corinthians 1:3–4), You know all that I am feeling, the pain, grief and the loss. *[Add anything else here that you are feeling.]* And all of these I bring to You.

Father, I thank You that You heal the broken-hearted and bind-up their wounds (Psalm 147:3) and ask that You heal all my wounds. I ask that You heal me of all the painful memories that I have.

Father, I give You all my despair and mourning and, in their place, I receive the oil of gladness and a garment of praise (Isaiah 61:3).

Thank You that I can come to You and cast all my cares on You.

In Jesus' name. Amen.

Prayer for the breaking of the power of words

In Jesus' name, I come against every word spoken against me by *[state here who the person/s were]* that is contrary to God's truth about me.

Father, forgive me for believing and accepting those words as truth and I repent of believing the lies of the evil one. I choose now to accept all Your truth of who I am.

Father, Your word says that words are like deadly arrows that are aimed against people (Psalm 64:3). In Jesus' name, I now pull out every negative word that has found its mark within me and ask for Your healing in all areas that I have been wounded.

In Jesus' name, I break the power of these words over my mind, body and spirit. I come against every curse that was directed against me and declare all its effects to be null and void over my life. I take the blood of the Lamb and cleanse myself from all defilement that these words brought in my life.

Father, I forgive *[person/s]* for saying *[state here what was said to you]*. I ask Your forgiveness for holding any bitterness, resentment or hatred *[add any other emotion that you have against them]* against *[person/s]*.

I now choose to bless *[person/s]* in all areas of their life/lives and release them from all my un-forgiveness, resentment and hatred *[or anything else you held against them]*.

I thank You, Lord Jesus, that by Your shed blood I have been set free.

In Jesus' name. Amen.

VOWS

Definition of a vow: a solemn promise or assertion; specifically: one by which a person is bound to an act, service, or condition.[2]

A vow can be spoken out loud, or it can be spoken within, called an inner vow. Once a vow is undertaken it sets the person on a course of action or pattern of behaviour, where they will be bound until the vow is confessed and repented.

Vows can be positive (e.g. like wedding vows) or negative. Here the prayer is for negative vows undertaken.

Prayers repenting of spoken or inner vows

Father God, I come before You and repent, renounce and ask Your forgiveness for making the vow of stating *[state here the vow you uttered or inwardly said]*.

I ask Your forgiveness for holding any anger, resentment, hatred *[add any sin here that comes to mind]* against *[insert name of person/s]* who spoke against me, prompting my rash vow. *[If applicable, as sometimes it is a situation that prompts us to make vows, not a person/s.]*

In Jesus' name, I now release myself from all the effects of this vow and ask that You cleanse me from all defilement. In Jesus' name, I declare that this vow will have no further effect over my mind, body or spirit.

---

2. https://www.merriam-webster.com/dictionary/vow

In Jesus' name, I break every agreement made with the enemy through making this vow. I command any evil spirit that would have attached itself to this vow, to leave me now, harmlessly, through my natural breathing.

Father God, I choose now to forgive *[person/s]* who spoke against me *[if applicable]* and release them from all my unforgiveness, resentment, hatred, etc. I choose now to bless them in all areas of their lives.

Heavenly Father, I thank You that through the shedding of the blood of Jesus I can be forgiven and cleansed. Praise His name.

In Jesus' name. Amen.

APPENDIX III
Scriptures

The word of God is living, powerful and sharper than any two-edged sword (Hebrews 4:12a). And we are told in Ephesians to use the sword of the Spirit which is the word of God. The scriptures are here for you to use as and when the Holy Spirit leads you. Memorising scriptures is excellent. Proclaiming the scriptures out loud is really good for building up faith, as Romans 10:17 tells us: *'So then faith comes by hearing, and hearing by the word of God.'*

Proclaim these verses when the enemy is harassing you and wield them as a sword, go on the offensive!

Speak the scriptures with faith. Believe in the word of the Lord, for Psalm 33:4 tells us: *'For the word of the LORD is right, and all His work is done in truth.'*

And finally, Proverbs 4:20–22: *'My son, give attention to my words; incline your ear to my sayings. Do not let them depart from your eyes; keep them in the midst of your heart; for they are life to those who find them, and health to all their flesh.'*

To be healthy we need the word of God!

Who we are in Christ

We need to know who we are and our position in Christ.

Having been born again, not of corruptible seed but incorruptible, through the word of God which lives and abides forever. (1 Peter 1:23)

In Him we have redemption through His blood, the forgiveness of sins, according to the riches of His grace. (Ephesians 1:7)

Therefore, if anyone is in Christ, he is a new creation; old things have passed away; behold, all things have become new. (2 Corinthians 5:17)

Or do you not know that your body is the temple of the Holy Spirit who is in you, whom you have from God, and you are not your own? (1 Corinthians 6:19)

He has delivered us from the power of darkness and conveyed us into the kingdom of the Son of His love. (Colossians 1:13)

Christ has redeemed us from the curse of the law, having become a curse for us (for it is written, 'Cursed is everyone who hangs on a tree'). (Galatians 3:13)

Just as He chose us in Him before the foundation of the world, that we should be holy and without blame before Him in love. (Ephesians 1:4)

Behold what manner of love the Father has bestowed on us, that we should be called children of God! Therefore the world does not know us, because it did not know Him. (1 John 3:1)

Yet in all these things we are more than conquerors through Him who loved us. (Romans 8:37)

You are the salt of the earth. You are the light of the world. (Matthew 5:13a, 14a)

Being justified freely by His grace through the redemption that is in Christ Jesus. (Romans 3:24)

Scriptures about believing

The importance of belief.

But let him ask in faith, with no doubting, for he who doubts is like a wave of the sea driven and tossed by the wind. (James 1:6)

And whatever things you ask in prayer, believing, you will receive. (Matthew 21:22)

If you can believe, all things are possible to him who believes. (Mark 9:23b)

Therefore I say to you, whatever things you ask when you pray, believe that you receive them, and you will have them. (Mark 11:24)

Beware, brethren, lest there be in any of you an evil heart of unbelief in departing from the living God. (Hebrews 3:12)

To the pure all things are pure, but to those who are defiled and unbelieving nothing is pure; but even their mind and conscience are defiled. (Titus 1:15)

For with the heart one believes unto righteousness, and with the mouth confession is made unto salvation. (Romans 10:10)

But without faith it is impossible to please Him, for he who comes to God must believe that He is, and that He is a rewarder of those who diligently seek Him. (Hebrews 11:6)

Scriptures to build faith

Use these verses when your faith needs building up. And remember, faith moves mountains (Mark 11:22–24)!

'Behold, I am the LORD, the God of all flesh. Is there anything too hard for Me?' (Jeremiah 32:27)

But Jesus looked at them and said to them, 'With men this is impossible, but with God all things are possible.' (Matthew 19:26)

Now to Him who is able to do exceedingly abundantly above all that we ask or think, according to the power that works in us. (Ephesians 3:20)

Then He touched their eyes, saying, 'According to your faith let it be to you.' (Matthew 9:29)

Now this is the confidence that we have in Him, that if we ask anything according to His will, He hears us. And if we know that He hears us, whatever we ask, we know that we have the petitions that we have asked of Him. (1 John 5:14–15)

For we walk by faith, not by sight. (2 Corinthians 5:7)

Above all, taking the shield of faith with which you will be able to quench all the fiery darts of the wicked one. (Ephesians 6:16)

And the prayer of faith will save the sick, and the Lord will raise him up. And if he has committed sins, he will be forgiven. (James 5:15)

Scriptures regarding fear

Use these scriptures when fear comes and keep using them until fear is gone.

For you did not receive the spirit of bondage again to fear, but you received the Spirit of adoption by whom we cry out, 'Abba, Father.' (Romans 8:15)

For God has not given us a spirit of fear, but of power and of love and of a sound mind. (2 Timothy 1:7)

The LORD is my light and my salvation; whom shall I fear? The LORD is the strength of my life; of whom shall I be afraid? (Psalm 27:1)

I sought the LORD, and He heard me, and delivered me from all my fears. (Psalm 34:4)

Fear not, for I am with you; be not dismayed, for I am your God. I will strengthen you, yes, I will help you, I will uphold you with My righteous right hand. (Isaiah 41:10)

For I, the LORD your God, will hold your right hand, saying to you, 'Fear not, I will help you.' (Isaiah 41:13)

But the very hairs of your head are all numbered. Do not fear therefore; you are of more value than many sparrows. (Luke 12:7)

Whenever I am afraid, I will trust in You. (Psalm 56:3)

Scriptures regarding anxiety

Use these when you are overwhelmed, till peace comes.

Be anxious for nothing, but in everything by prayer and supplication, with thanksgiving, let your requests be made known to God; and the peace of God, which surpasses all understanding, will guard your hearts and minds through Christ Jesus. (Philippians 4:6–7)

Peace I leave with you, My peace I give to you; not as the world gives do I give to you. Let not your heart be troubled, neither let it be afraid. (John 14:27)

In the multitude of my anxieties within me, Your comforts delight my soul. (Psalm 94:19)

Casting all your care upon Him, for He cares for you. (1 Peter 5:7)

Come to Me, all you who labour and are heavy laden, and I will give you rest. (Matthew 11:28)

Cast your burden on the LORD, and He shall sustain you; He shall never permit the righteous to be moved. (Psalm 55:22)

Therefore do not worry about tomorrow, for tomorrow will worry about its own things. Sufficient for the day is its own trouble. (Matthew 6:34)

Let not your heart be troubled; you believe in God, believe also in Me. (John 14:1)

Why are you cast down, O my soul? And why are you disquieted within me? Hope in God, for I shall yet praise Him for the help of His countenance. (Psalm 42:5)

LORD, *You will establish peace for us, for You have also done all our works in us.* (Isaiah 26:12)

Scriptures about trust

These scriptures tell us the blessings that come with trusting the Lord. If we do not trust the Lord then the opposite can happen.

Blessed is that man who makes the LORD his trust, and does not respect the proud, nor such as turn aside to lies. (Psalm 40:4)

Trust in the LORD with all your heart, and lean not on your own understanding; in all your ways acknowledge Him, and He shall direct your paths. (Proverbs 3:5–6)

Behold, God is my salvation, I will trust and not be afraid; 'For YAH, the LORD, is my strength and song; He also has become my salvation. (Isaiah 12:2)

Trust in the LORD forever, for in YAH, the LORD, is everlasting strength. (Isaiah 26:4)

But I have trusted in Your mercy; my heart shall rejoice in Your salvation. (Psalm 13:5)

You will keep him in perfect peace, whose mind is stayed on You, because he trusts in You. (Isaiah 26:3)

Blessed is the man who trusts in the LORD, and whose hope is the LORD. (Jeremiah 17:7)

And those who know Your name will put their trust in You; for You, LORD, have not forsaken those who seek You. (Psalm 9:10)

Some trust in chariots, and some in horses; but we will remember the name of the LORD our God. (Psalm 20:7)

Now may the God of hope fill you with all joy and peace in believing, that you may abound in hope by the power of the Holy Spirit. (Romans 15:13)

Thus says the LORD: 'Cursed is the man who trusts in man and makes flesh his strength, whose heart departs from the LORD.' (Jeremiah 17:5)

The fear of man brings a snare, but whoever trusts in the LORD shall be safe. (Proverbs 29:25)

He who trusts in his riches will fall, but the righteous will flourish like foliage. (Proverbs 11:28)

It is better to trust in the LORD than to put confidence in man. (Psalm 118:8)

Scriptures about forgiveness

Why we have to forgive.

Bearing with one another, and forgiving one another, if anyone has a complaint against another; even as Christ forgave you, so you also must do. (Colossians 3:13)

For if you forgive men their trespasses, your heavenly Father will also forgive you. But if you do not forgive men their trespasses, neither will your Father forgive your trespasses. (Matthew 6:14–15)

Take heed to yourselves. If your brother sins against you, rebuke him; and if he repents, forgive him. And if he sins against you seven times in a day, and seven times in a day returns to you, saying, 'I repent,' you shall forgive him. (Luke 17:3–4)

And be kind to one another, tenderhearted, forgiving one another, just as God in Christ forgave you. (Ephesians 4:32)

If we confess our sins, He is faithful and just to forgive us our sins and to cleanse us from all unrighteousness. (1 John 1:9)

In Him we have redemption through His blood, the forgiveness of sins, according to the riches of His grace. (Ephesians 1:7)

And whenever you stand praying, if you have anything against anyone, forgive him, that your Father in heaven may also forgive you your trespasses. (Mark 11:25)

And his master was angry, and delivered him to the torturers until he should pay all that was due to him. So My heavenly Father also will do to you if each of you, from his heart, does not forgive his brother his trespasses. (Matthew 18:34–35)

Then Peter came to Him and said, 'Lord, how often shall my brother sin against me, and I forgive him? Up to seven times?' Jesus said to him, 'I do not say to you, up to seven times, but up to seventy times seven.' (Matthew 18:21–22)